Dear Reader:

The book you are about to read is the latest bestseller from the St. Martin's True Crime Library, the imprint the *New York Times* calls "the leader in true crime!" Each month, we offer you a fascinating account of the latest, most sensational crime that has captured the national attention. St. Martin's is the publisher of bestselling true crime author and crime journalist Kieran Crowley, who explores the dark, deadly links between a prominent Manhattan surgeon and the disappearance of his wife fifteen years earlier in THE SURGEON'S WIFE. Suzy Spencer's BREAKING POINT guides readers through the tortuous twists and turns in the case of Andrea Yates, the Houston mother who drowned her five young children in the family's bathtub. In Edgar Award-nominated DARK DREAMS, legendary FBI profiler Roy Hazelwood and bestselling crime author Stephen G. Michaud shine light on the inner workings of America's most violent and depraved murderers. In the book you now hold, THE PREACHER'S SON, Lynn Chandler-Willis takes an in-depth look at a marriage that appeared to be perfect—but hid a wall of lies . . .

St. Martin's True Crime Library gives you the stories behind the headlines. Our authors take you right to the scene of the crime and into the minds of the most notorious murderers to show you what really makes them tick. St. Martin's True Crime Library paperbacks are better than the most terrifying thriller, because it's all true! The next time you want a crackling good read, make sure it's got the St. Martin's True Crime Library logo on the spine—you'll be up all night!

Charles E. Spicer, Jr.
Executive Editor, St. Martin's True Crime Library

"We've Got Flames!"

Suddenly, fireman Alan Fields saw a red-orange glow through the smoke in the hallway, just beyond the bedroom. "We've got flames!" he shouted. He knocked the remaining shards of glass from the window and crawled through, pulling the hose with him.

While a two-man crew went through the window, Alan and his line crew pushed their way into the kitchen. The fans had vented little of the smoke but enough to let them enter.

Although slight of build, Alan had no trouble wrestling the heavy hose and its explosive power as the pressurized water blasted relief to the peeling walls. He pulled the line through the kitchen, the living room, into the hallway. Smoke-grayed insulation and disintegrating Sheetrock littered the floor.

The flames seen earlier were already extinguished. But the smoke was still so thick, Alan could only see inches ahead. All of a sudden, the floor was no longer there. He had come upon the hole so quickly, all he could do was fall.

A four-foot hole had burned through the flooring, dumping a mound of smoldering debris into the crawl space beneath the house. Alan rolled off the heated mound and brushed pieces of the debris aside. But the bulk of it didn't move.

It was too hard to be insulation. Too soft to be a floor joist.

"Oh no," Alan mumbled. Fighting to keep his composure, he yelled up to the others. "We've got a body!"

THE PREACHER'S SON

A TRUE STORY OF MURDER IN NORTH CAROLINA

(previously titled *Unholy Covenant*)

LYNN CHANDLER-WILLIS

St. Martin's Paperbacks

The Preacher's Son was previously published under the title *Unholy Covenant*.

Published by arrangement with Addicus Books

THE PREACHER'S SON

Cover photograph of wedding courtesy Lloyd's Photography.

ISBN: 0-312-97807-3

Printed in the United States of America

St. Martin's Paperbacks edition / May 2003

10 9 8 7 6 5 4 3 2 1

For my dad and mom,
Willie and Willie Mae Chandler,
who I know, somewhere over that rainbow,
are smiling down on me.

ACKNOWLEDGMENTS

A great many people helped me tell this story. I am forever grateful for their openness, their honesty, and their trust in me.

I am forever grateful to the Blakley family. Sheila, Richard, Reuben, Kristy, and "Grandma" Bertha welcomed me into their hearts and their homes. Often, the memories they shared were painful. I thank them for reliving these memories and revisiting a time they wish to forget.

I thank all the men and women of the Guilford County Sheriff's Department who helped me tell this story. Special thanks to Sheriff B.J. Barnes and the Major Crimes Unit—four of the hardest-working men I've ever met. My thanks, too, to Detective Sergeant David L. DeBerry for helping me understand the incredible amount of work that goes into a homicide case. I thank Detective Jim Church for telling me his story and making his notes available. I also express my gratitude to Detective Steve McBride, a fellow Irishman, and Detective Herb Byrd. To District III

Detective Sergeant John N. Davis, I thank you for always taking the time to listen or answer even the simplest of questions.

I also thank State Bureau of Investigation Special Agent Harold Pendergrass, Guilford County Assistant District Attorney Richard Panosh, Ann Mauney of the North Carolina Department of Insurance, and Herman McCauley of McCauley Investigative Services, Inc.

My gratitude goes out to the Pleasant Garden Fire Department—especially to Alan Fields, Benny Shaw, and Deputy Chief Dale Marley—who enlightened me about fire fighting. I also thank Pete Cooper and all the other regulars at Brown's Ol' Opry for giving me a place to relax.

My thanks to Julie Parks, Doug Hewitt, Mary Elizabeth Parker, and Michelle Olson—all fellow members of the Writer's Group of the Triad—for their months of encouragement. Thanks to Rod Colvin of Addicus Books for his patience and support of this project.

And to the fine folks of Pleasant Garden—from Marion's Corner Mart to the Pleasant Garden Drug Store and everyone in between—I thank you for your encouragement.

Last but not least, I thank my family. Without your support, this book would not have been possible. To my sister, Rae Locklear, thanks for always being there. To my son and daughter, Garey and Nina Willis, thank you for your unlimited, unselfish sacrifices while Mom pursued her dream. The only way I can repay you is to give you the wings to pursue your own.

AUTHOR'S NOTES

Like other residents of Pleasant Garden, I lived this story. I knew a lot about the case from the start. Still, it took many hours of interviews with family members, friends, and investigators to accurately recreate the events. Some scenes are re-creations of their memories; some are based on cold, hard facts taken from court testimony. The names of some characters in the book have been changed to protect their privacy.

In the beginning, I wanted to write this story simply because I found it fascinating and sad. Yet it became something more—a journey of self-discovery.

William Shakespeare once wrote: "This above all, to thine own self be true." One should never have to change or sacrifice one's life to suit the desires of another. Manipulation and intimidation can be destructive. I hope this book will help others find the strength within themselves to never be anyone's victim.

THE PREACHER'S SON

CHAPTER ONE

Who through faith conquered kingdoms, administered justice, and gained what was promised; who shut the mouths of lions, quenched the fury of the flames, and escaped the edge of the sword.

Hebrews 11: 33–34

October 9, 1995 8:40 P.M.

Richard Blakley took off his shoes and wiggled his toes. His feet were tired. They were always tired this time of night. Maintaining BP's fuel pumps was tiring enough, but the hour-and-a-half daily drive from Pleasant Garden, North Carolina, to Raleigh, the state's capital, wore him out.

Richard had just settled into his worn recliner when lights flashed through the window. He heard a truck engine running and waited for it to shut off, but it didn't.

His daughter-in-law, Kristy Blakley, burst through

the back door. "You've got to come! Now!" she screamed. Her narrow cheeks were flushed and reddened with tears. "Hurry! There's no time."

"Kristy, what's the—"

"Hurry!" she screamed, all ninety pounds of her pushing Richard outside to the waiting truck.

"At least let me get my shoes." Richard turned back toward the house, but Kristy grabbed his arm.

"No! There's no time! We've got to go now!" Her words were clipped, escaping between gasps and sobs.

This wasn't like Kristy at all. She seldom let excitement, good or bad, overrule her quiet, reserved nature.

Richard slapped the seat belt around himself as the pickup gained momentum. He braced his hand across the roof of the truck since Kristy wasn't slowing for the potholes that canyoned the private road. "Honey, we're not going to be any good to anyone if we don't get there in one piece."

Kristy wiped the back of her small hand against her cheek but didn't respond.

"Kristy, please tell me what's the matter," Richard begged, his voice rising with fear.

Her knuckles were white from gripping the wheel, her eyes fixed on the gravel road ahead. As she turned off Branchwater Road onto Highway 22, she yanked the truck back into the right lane.

Dusk had already fallen. The acres of farmland and pasture along Highway 22 blended into the outline of trees and woods. The porch lights of neighbors' houses, people Richard had known all his life, glared like fireflies as the truck raced by.

"It's . . . it's . . . Patricia," Kristy finally stuttered. "There's a fire."

Richard's heart stopped. Fear clamped it like a vise, then gradually released its hold, allowing the fright to spread through his body like a fast-growing cancer.

"Patricia . . ." It was the only word he could say as thoughts of his only daughter raced through his mind.

Even through the darkness, Richard could see ominous black smoke roiling from the chimney and seeping from the vents of his daughter's ranch-style home. He prayed it was all just a bad dream, that the smoke was really just a thick fog clouding his perception.

Richard's son, Reuben Blakley, rushed to meet them in the front yard. "I think Patricia's inside, Daddy. I think she's in there." Reuben bent over, gasping for breath, crying. Kristy grabbed her husband's hand and squeezed it tightly.

In his stocking feet, Richard ran from window to window of the gray-sided house, pounding on the white-hot glass, screaming his daughter's name.

Twenty-four-year-old Alan Fields buckled his helmet and leapt from the jump seat of the fire engine. An uneasy feeling gripped Alan, a six-year veteran of the Pleasant Garden Fire Department, when he heard dispatch's second call. Dispatch said someone may be trapped inside. Dispatch's first call had confirmed that it was Ted and Patricia Kimble's house. Theirs was the only house on Brandon Station Court. Now, as Alan eyed Patricia's car in the driveway, he feared the worst.

Alan knew Ted and Patricia well. He had gone to

school with Ted; he had dated Patricia's cousin. At times like this, he wished he were a paid fireman assigned to another department. Maybe one not so close to home.

Thick smoke poured from the vents, growing blacker, more threatening. Alan grabbed the preconnect hose and jerked it into the carport. Two other firemen joined him on the line and waited as Alan tested the back door. Even through his gloves, the door was hot, almost scorching, but it pushed open easily.

Instantly, as Alan entered the house, searing heat and blinding smoke enveloped him. "Good God!" he yelled. Never in his career had Alan felt such intense heat.

Crouching, Alan and the two other firemen moved forward, struggling against the thick smoke as if it were quicksand. But the heat was just too much. Alan motioned the men backward, praying they could see him through the smoke.

Outside, Alan jerked his mask off and gulped fresh air. Sweat cascaded down his forehead and stung his eyes. "Smoke's too thick," he puffed. "We're gonna have to use the fans."

A large crowd began to gather on the front lawn. They huddled together near the street, uncertainty, panic, and horror etched into their faces. Several were members of Patricia's family. Others, like Alan, had gone to school with Ted or Patricia or knew them through church. Pleasant Garden was a tight-knit community. A community people seldom left. Those who did leave always came back, sooner or later.

Alan looked back at the smoldering house, the hellhole from which he had come. If Patricia was inside, there was no way in heaven she could still be alive. Tragedies like this weren't supposed to happen in Pleasant Garden. Especially to someone as good as Patricia Blakley Kimble.

On the front side of the house, another fireman smashed the window of the master bedroom with a metal rod and reached through the shattered glass. He groped anything his hand landed upon, hoping a body might be within his reach.

Suddenly, he saw a red-orange glow through the smoke in the hallway, just beyond the bedroom. "We've got flames!" he shouted. He knocked the remaining shards of glass from the window and crawled through, pulling the hose with him.

While a two-man crew went through the window, Alan and his line crew pushed their way into the kitchen. The fans had vented little of the smoke but enough to let them enter.

Although slight of build, Alan had no trouble wrestling the heavy hose and its explosive power as the pressurized water blasted relief to the peeling walls. He pulled the line through the kitchen, the living room, into the hallway. Smoke-grayed insulation and disintegrating Sheetrock littered the floor.

The flames seen earlier were already extinguished. But the smoke was still so thick, Alan could only see inches ahead. All of a sudden, the floor was no longer there. He had come upon the hole so quickly, all he could do was fall.

A four-foot hole had burned through the flooring, dumping a mound of smoldering debris into the crawl space beneath the house. Alan rolled off the heated mound and brushed pieces of the debris aside. But the bulk of it didn't move.

It was too hard to be insulation. Too soft to be a floor joist.

"Oh no," Alan mumbled. Fighting to keep his composure, he yelled up to the others. "We've got a body!"

CHAPTER TWO

On October 9, 1995, Detective Jim Church was working an off-duty uniform assignment at the Southern Auto Auction when he received the page. The managers of the auction had known beforehand that Church was on call. They also knew his responsibilities to the Major Crimes Unit of the Guilford County Sheriff's Department came first.

Although a fifteen-year veteran, Church had come to the Sheriff's Department later in life than most. Now, at forty-nine, his sand-brown hair had begun to show flecks of gray around his temples. He fretted about the thought of an expanding waistline despite his well-trimmed six-foot frame.

Church hailed from North Carolina's Blue Ridge Mountains and carried the slow, easy manner with him when he uprooted and headed for Guilford County, located in the north-central part of the state. He was a meticulous thinker, choosing to fully evaluate a situation before acting or even speaking. He spoke in soft words accented by a thick Southern drawl.

Church scribbled down the address from Communications. *Pleasant Garden?* Not much in the way of serious crimes ever happened in Pleasant Garden. He cranked the engine of the Chevrolet Lumina and headed south.

The address sounded familiar: 2104 Brandon Station Court. But in his fifteen years with the department, he had heard a lot of addresses. Still, the fact he was headed toward Pleasant Garden bothered him.

Pleasant Garden just wasn't known for its crimes. It had its share of occasional burglaries, a property crime now and then, but serious crimes just weren't part of its character. Tucked into the southeast corner of Guilford County, the small rural community was better known for its churches and championship little league baseball teams.

The 4,000 residents of Pleasant Garden were a diverse lot. Farmers whose ancestors helped to settle the area lived next door to transplanted northern business executives who wanted their children raised in a back-to-basics environment. The town lay about five miles south of Greensboro, a city whose expanding population brimmed at well over 100,000.

Greensboro, the county seat, had in the past been quick to annex areas with a promising tax base. Fearing the loss of their village-like atmosphere, rumbles of incorporation spread through Pleasant Garden, dominating barbershop conversations. The folks of Pleasant Garden liked their simple way of life just fine. They didn't need, nor want, big-city conveniences or the trouble that often came with them.

Church saw the glow of lights above the treetops as he neared Brandon Station Court. Suddenly, he remembered. He had investigated a burglary at the address a few years ago. He remembered the house because it was the only house on the small court, almost an afterthought in a new subdivision. He couldn't, however, remember the homeowner's name. She was a young girl, much younger than most homeowners. She was sweet, too. *Baker? Blake?* It would come to him eventually.

He carefully navigated his car through the fire trucks and the crowd of people lining the street. Yellow tape corralled off most of the yard, keeping the spectators at a distance. Some of the firemen were already securing their equipment, their soot-covered faces long and downcast.

Church's supervisor, Detective Sergeant David DeBerry, was standing near a gazebo in the front yard. A small crowd of people gathered around him. Only forty-four, DeBerry had been with the Guilford County Sheriff's Department twenty-four years. He had spent only a few short years as a patrol officer before exchanging his uniform for the coat and tie of a detective.

Tall and handsome with a head of auburn curls he kept cut short, DeBerry's cockeyed grin could charm the sergeant into, or out of, most any situation. His interview skills unmatched, he had been called not only by his peers, but also by prosecutors and defense attorneys alike, one of, if not *the*, best homicide investigators in the state.

Church ducked under the tape and headed toward the house. The usually crisp October air was heavy with an acrid stench. A volunteer fireman himself, Church was used to the smell of a burnt structure. Even the putrid smell of burnt flesh.

He gave his name to the accountability officer and entered the house. "Good gosh," Church said, waving his hand in the smothering heat as if he could shoo it away like a bothersome fly.

The kitchen was in shambles. Utensils, silverware, broken dishes were strewn about the flooded floor. What remained of the buckled walls was smoked black.

The living room had fared little better. Distorted photographs of a beautiful, brown-haired young woman smiled through warped and melted picture frames. Framed words of inspiration and cross-stitched Bible verses lay scattered on the floor.

The *click-click* of the Crime Lab's camera came in a steady, staccato rhythm as the technician moved from one room to another. Investigators with the Fire Marshall's office grouped together and evaluated the scene. A handful of firemen milled about, waiting for direction from the fire marshall. Thin, smoky gray outlines circled their faces where their face masks had been but did little to conceal their weariness.

It's going to be a long night, Church thought.

DeBerry approached from behind, his loafers sloshing through the water that saturated the carpet. "What do you think?" he asked Church.

Church pointed to the kitchen, then followed an obvious trail with his finger. The burn pattern began in the kitchen, snaked its way into the living room over the back of the sofa, and continued into the hallway. He had seen enough fires to recognize a blatant pour pattern when he saw one.

DeBerry had seen the same thing. "Yep. One of the firemen found a gas can in the kitchen."

"Odd place to keep a gas can."

"Wonder the damn thing didn't melt." DeBerry wiped a stream of sweat from his brow and tugged at his tie. The heat inside the house was still stifling.

A commotion outside the living-room window drew the detectives' attention. A heavyset woman fell to the ground and wailed uncontrollably. A young man bent over her, locked his arms underneath hers, and struggled to hoist the woman up.

"That's the husband, Ted Kimble, and his mother Edna," said DeBerry.

Church watched as the young man tried desperately to lead his mother to a waiting car. The woman resisted, crying out, reaching toward the house, her face twisted in disbelief.

"I asked the family to gather at their church," DeBerry said. "I want to keep as many as we can away from the scene."

"Have you talked to them yet?"

"A little bit. I told them we'd come down to the church in a few minutes."

"Who called 911?" Church asked, turning away from the scene outside.

"The brother of the woman who lived here. His name's Reuben Blakley."

Blakley. Church was almost certain that was the name of the young girl he had met a few years ago. "Where was the husband?"

"Work." DeBerry walked into the hallway and

lifted a ladder that had been used to bridge the burned-out hole. Church followed. Both detectives stooped beside the gaping hole to get a better look.

"The fire was so hot it burned a hole around the body, and the body fell through to the crawl space." DeBerry said.

"It didn't burn this hot anywhere else?"

DeBerry shook his head. "Nope. Whoever that is, they were doused pretty good."

The body was face down, completely charred, the left foot and lower right leg burnt completely away. The arms were raised above the head. A small patch of fabric clung to the left arm.

Church studied the arms for a moment. When death by fire is imminent, the body's natural instinct is to draw itself into a fetal position. Whoever this victim was, fire wasn't the killer.

"We're going to be here awhile on this one," DeBerry said as he stood. He replaced the ladder across the hole and shimmied over it. "Come look at the bedroom."

The master bedroom was ransacked. Still, it wasn't difficult to tell what disarray was the firemen's doings and what wasn't. The firemen had left no obvious pattern.

Dresser drawers had been pulled out and stacked neatly one on top of the other. A twenty dollar bill sat atop a stack of other untouched bills in the corner of the top drawer. Bits and pieces of jewelry were equally undisturbed.

"Someone did a piss-poor job of staging this, didn't they?" Church said. Unlike the previous burglary he had investigated at the residence, this one obviously wasn't real. Burglars seldom took the time to neatly stack dresser drawers, nor did they often leave behind visible cash.

Maybe the victim had walked in on a burglary? No, Church thought, if the victim was the same girl who lived here before, she would have never entered the house if she suspected something wasn't right. She had been much too frightened, too cautious. "The girl that lived here, what was her name?" Church asked DeBerry as memories of his conversations with the young woman ran through this mind.

"Patricia Kimble."

"Hey, you guys ready to remove the body?" the fire marshall called into the bedroom.

"You got everything you need?" DeBerry asked one of the Crime Lab techs hovering over the dresser drawers. The tech waved the sergeant on indicating he had all the pictures of the hallway he needed.

Down in the hole, two firemen scooted a sheet underneath the body and handed up the corners. Church stared at what was once a person and hoped this time his memory was wrong. Wrong about a sweet girl named Patricia.

He grabbed a corner of the sheet and helped carry the body out to the carport. The fire department's floodlights cast an overzealous illumination, severely shadowing the area in spots. Church bent over the sheet and gazed down at the charred remains. He scanned the body up and down, zeroing in on the back of the skull. He glanced up at DeBerry, who had noticed the same thing. The sergeant slowly nodded.

"You ready to take a ride over to the church?" DeBerry asked.

Church looked back over the body, then stood. He stared at the back of the victim's skull.

As they walked to the car, DeBerry fished a cigarette from his shirt pocket. "You noticed it too, huh?" he said, referring to the small hole in the back of the victim's skull.

"At least she died quick."

The contrast between the well-lit, busy atmosphere of Brandon Station Court and the darkened, sleepy heart of Pleasant Garden was as stark as the shadows cast by the floodlights. It was close to eleven o'clock and Pleasant Garden had long ago called it a night. The lonely whistle of a train could be heard through the silence as it chugged along the tracks that ran parallel to Pleasant Garden Road. Marion's Corner Mart, located at the corner of Pleasant Garden Road and Spur Road, had closed its doors around nine o'clock. If anyone needed milk or bread, they'd have to either wait until morning or drive the five miles into Greensboro. Most folks would wait.

The little strip shopping center, with its competing beauty shops, a TV repair shop, a florist, and a barbershop, had closed several hours earlier. The town's only two factories, Hooker Furniture and Boren Brick, operated skeleton crews at night. Their parking lots were nearly empty.

The people of Pleasant Garden prided themselves on family values and a simple way of life. A life that had roots as deep as the centuries-old oak trees that lined Pleasant Garden Road. With its Baptist church on one corner, its Methodist church on the other, and the elementary school sandwiched in between, Pleasant Garden was as wholesome as a little town could be.

Or it once was, Church thought.

DeBerry pulled into the parking lot of South Elm Street Baptist Church, just a few miles north of the heart of Pleasant Garden. Aside from Pleasant Garden Baptist, South Elm Street was one of the larger churches in the area. The building sat in the middle of cleared, well-manicured acreage. On any given Sunday, the paved parking lot was brimming with cars. As it was now.

"I know they're not having services at this time of night," Church said, glancing over at the array of cars and pickups filling the parking lot.

"I think they're all friends and family of Patricia's."

DeBerry parked. He and Church hustled up the steps of the fellowship hall.

Never before had Church seen so many people gathered in a similar situation. Folding metal chairs had been set out. Few were empty. Church gazed over the sea of faces, each flushed red, their eyes hollowed with shock.

The woman Church had watched earlier through the living-room window, Edna Kimble, sat alone, staring blankly ahead. She looked out of place. Her expensive dress, gold jewelry, and designer haircut separated her from the faded jeans and sweatshirts of the others.

"We're here to see Ted Kimble," DeBerry told Benny Shaw, a 911 dispatch operator whom both DeBerry and Church had known for years.

Shaw was a large man. While most men in the area wore some type of ball cap, Shaw always wore a longshoreman's cap. It fit his bearlike exterior well. But Shaw was a kind soul with soft, gentle eyes. Aside from his duties with 911, he was a volunteer with the Pleasant Garden Fire Department. And Patricia's godfather.

He had been on duty at 911 when the call came in to communication headquarters. He waited anxiously for news from the firefighters on the scene. Some news, any news. Just tell him it wasn't real. Tell him it was a false alarm and Patricia was okay.

But when they called back and said they had found a body, gentle Benny, his heart in his throat, got up from his seat. He told his supervisors he was going, he had to leave. They could fire him if they wanted.

"Ted's in the sanctuary with the pastor," Shaw said, his voice nearly cracking. "I'll go get him."

While DeBerry and Church waited, DeBerry bobbed his head in the direction opposite of Edna Kimble. "The man and woman over there, that's Patricia's parents. Richard and Sheila Blakley. That's Patricia's brother Reuben and his wife Kristy between them."

A large crowd of people surrounded the Blakleys, some holding one another's hands, some with their heads bent and eyes closed as their mouths moved in silent prayer.

Richard Blakley sat beside his mother, total shock engraved deeply into his face. He was a large man, well over six feet, but the deep, hooded eyes that were now streaked red contradicted his manly size. His mother Bertha was a tiny woman. She sat clutching her purse with one hand and holding her son's hand with the other. A young man knelt beside her and wailed loudly. He rested his head in her lap as he stroked her arm. The display of emotion appeared to make her uncomfortable. She tried on occasion to move away from the young man, but he persisted in sharing his grief.

Moments later, Shaw returned with the reverend. "I've told Ted to wait in my study," the pastor said. "You'll have more privacy there."

Church and DeBerry followed him down a darkened, narrow hallway. The reverend rapped once on one of the doors, then slowly opened it.

Church got his first good look at Theodore Mead Kimble. He was a young man, Church assumed probably mid-twenties, with a stocky build. The sleeves of his navy-blue T-shirt bulged at his biceps. His eyes were the color of jade and as piercing as they were bright. His concrete jaw was round and full and sat firmly on top of a too-thick neck. Dark brown curls, cut short and well above his neckline, framed his round face.

"Ted, this is Detective Church," DeBerry said as he closed the door. "We need to ask you a couple of questions."

Ted glanced at Church and nodded.

"Ted," Church began, speaking clearly and firmly, "there was a body found in the house. We don't know yet if it was your wife or not."

Ted batted his eyes and looked away from the detectives.

"Ted, did you have any guns in the house?" Church asked.

"Yeah," he said, his voice nearly cracking. He cleared his throat then continued. "I have three."

"What are they? Do you recall?"

"A .45 caliber Glock, a Remington 1100 semiautomatic shotgun, and a 300 Win-Mag."

A 300 Win-Mag? An incredibly high-powered and expensive rifle, the firearm was used mostly by professional hunters for big-game hunting. There were few, if any, game in North Carolina large enough to warrant use of such a rifle.

"You a hunter?" Church asked.

Ted shook his head.

"What about other valuables?" Church continued.

"I'm cold."

"Pardon?"

"I'm cold. I'm real cold." He rubbed his thick fingers over his arms and shivered. DeBerry handed him a thin blanket that had been lying in the corner of the office. Ted draped it around his shoulders, then stared at Church. "I'm sorry, what was the question again?"

"Did you have any other valuables in the house?"

Ted shrugged and shook his head. "Not really."

"Does your wife have any medical conditions that you're aware of?"

Again, Ted shook his head.

"Who is her medical doctor?"

"Pleasant Garden Family Practice."

"What about her dentist?"

"Dr. Worland on Tabernacle Church Road."

"When was the last time you saw your wife, Ted?"

"Noon, maybe." He pulled the blanket tighter around his shoulders and shifted his weight. He spoke in a matter-of-fact voice and answered the questions quickly, as if they needed no thought or consideration. "We had lunch together. She got off work early and—"

"Where does she work?"

"Cinnamon Ridge Apartments. She was the manager."

Was?

"She got off work early and was going to go home and mow the yard. Then she had prayer meeting here at the church, but she never showed, so I got concerned."

"Were you supposed to meet her here at the church?"

"No, I was at work. But I couldn't get her on the phone at home, so I tried here. I couldn't get an answer here either, so I started getting worried."

"So what did you do when you couldn't get her?" DeBerry asked, wondering if Ted's answer would be similar to what Reuben Blakley had told him earlier.

"I called her brother, Reuben, and asked him to go over to the house and see if everything was okay."

DeBerry glanced at Church to continue.

"Ted, we always ask this question in this situation, okay?" Church said.

Ted glanced up at the detectives, staring at each one, then again looked away. "Sure."

"Does your wife have any life insurance?"

Ted glanced at DeBerry, then Church. He tightened his grip on the blanket. "Yeah, we have two."

"Do you know right off what they're worth?"

Ted cleared his throat. "Well, we actually only have one. We canceled the other. She's got one through work, and I didn't think we needed another one."

"How much is it worth?" Church repeated.

"Which one?"

"You said you only had the one," DeBerry reminded him.

"Oh—it was fifty thousand. No, wait a minute, maybe it was a hundred thousand. I'm not sure." Ted yawned.

CHAPTER THREE

I was talking with the Lord and I kept thinking I'm just afraid to be without a husband—the Lord opened my eyes to the fact that he had been preparing me for the role to be a wife. This promised me that I'd be married some day. I truly believe that now! I was talking with a friend a few months ago about Ted and he quoted the saying that if you love something, let it go—if it comes back, it was yours. If it doesn't, then it never was. Well, I told him that I just wanted to make sure Ted was mine before I let him go.

Patricia Kimble's journal
September 7, 1992

May 7, 1994

Patricia Blakley gazed at her reflection in the full-length mirror and softly smiled. Her wedding gown fit well. The princess seams accentuated her slender waist, and the scalloped bodice slightly hinted at the swell of her breasts. Her smile turned downward into a concerned frown. "Grandma, you don't think this . . . shows too much, do you?" With trembling hands, Patricia tugged at the beaded neckline.

Bertha Blakley looked at her granddaughter's reflection in the mirror and chuckled. "Honey, you look like a perfect lady. Ted's a very lucky man."

Patricia's frown quickly disappeared, and her radiant smile returned. "No, I'm the lucky one. I'm about to marry the man I truly, truly love. The Lord has blessed us both so much."

For Ted Kimble, life's blessings hadn't always come easy, though.

Ted was the eldest son of a struggling young minister. Money had always been scarce for the Kimbles. For years, the family lived in a single-wide mobile home in a trailer park on the outskirts of Pleasant Garden. Ted and his younger brother, Ronnie Jr., learned early on the rewards of hard work and the value of a dollar. And Ted learned the benefits of charm. He was well liked by the neighborhood kids, especially the girls, who quivered at the mere sight of his smile.

Ted was everything Ronnie wasn't. While Ted was confident, to the point of arrogance, Ronnie struggled with the awkwardness of youth. Ted was dominating, the one to always lead; Ronnie was forever the follower. Ted was calculating, one to think everything through; Ronnie was easily excitable, one to dive in head first. Where Ted had the grace and reserve of a strong, sturdy mountain lion, Ronnie was the lop-eared, lolling-tongue, eager-to-please puppy.

In high school, although Ted had the build for athletics, he had no time for sports. His grades were marginal and he had no desire for college, but he did have a deep-set desire to succeed. It was almost a driving need, a need to have one dollar more. One dollar more could buy a nice car to replace the outdated, oil-blowing family sedan. It could buy a nice house, a real house instead of a trailer, a dream house with lots of rooms, twelve-foot ceilings, and floor-to-roof windows.

Instead of spending time in after-school activities like other teenagers, Ted took a part-time job at Lyles' Building Supplies. Gary Lyles, the owner, was a member of Monnett Road Baptist Church where Ted's father, Ron Kimble Sr., was now pastor. Lyles had taken an immediate liking to Ted. He was so impressed with the boy's work ethics and determination, Lyles, looking forward to retirement, groomed Ted to take over the business.

Barely into his twenties, it looked liked Ted Kimble had it all. Still, something was missing.

Between work and church, the fellowship of other Christians employed much of his social life. But his father's church was small, most of the members older. He began visiting South Elm Street Baptist Church, a larger church where many of his friends from school went. He already knew many of the young people who attended the church and had dated several of the girls. One girl he didn't know. Patricia Blakley.

Like some kind of unexplained cosmic force—something better left unanswered—Patricia Blakley knew the moment she first saw him that she would one day be Mrs. Theodore Mead Kimble.

Now, standing in the nursery of Monnett Road Baptist Church, the soft sounds of a harp filtering under the closed door, Patricia's heart fluttered in her chest. In a few moments, she would walk down the aisle. In a few moments, she would vow to love, honor, and obey the man that God himself had sent her.

At twenty-six, Patricia Gail Blakley had worried that her wedding day might never come. Most of her friends from school and church were already married. Some had even started families. She was glad, though, that she had waited until she found someone who loved God as much as she did. It was hard for those who weren't saved to understand the commitment a faithful Christian makes to Jesus Christ. She wondered if perhaps her own mother and father might still be together had they let God lead their marriage.

Patricia wondered if her mother had ever felt the way about her father that she felt about Ted? Trembling when he touched her? Smiling for no other reason than the thought of him? She felt sure her parents had loved each other at some point. Certainly, they had cared for and longed for the other.

Their divorce was so bitter, though. Filled with cutting words and biting anger. Although Patricia had already moved away from home when it happened, it still hurt her to see her parents so angry with one another. What had gone wrong? Patricia had tried but really couldn't put her finger on it.

When she was a child, everything had seemed so normal, like any other family. Her dad worked as an electrician and a locksmith. Sometimes he drove a delivery truck. Her mom worked in a factory. Between her mom and grandma, dinner was always cooked, clothes were always darned, and their house, although small, was always filled with plenty of laughter and love.

In elementary school, although she and Reuben had plenty of friends, most of their playtime was spent with their cousins who lived next door. Poor Reuben—he was the only little boy amongst Patricia and their cousins. If he wanted to play, he had to play school. Patricia was always the teacher. With a firm hand planted on her tiny hip, she would instruct her "class."

In *real* school, Patricia was a good student and had an uncanny knack for math. By the time she was sixteen, she had applied her knowledge of numbers to her personal life so well, she had saved enough money from a part-time job to buy her own car. By the time she was twenty-three, she had saved enough for a down payment on a home. While most young people her age had yet to leave the nest, Patricia was a homeowner.

But she wasn't "bookish" about numbers and would choose a good physical activity over a ledger column any time. She was offered a bookkeeping job at a grocery store but chose a stocking position instead. She just wasn't content unless she was moving. Patricia often worked two jobs to kill idle time.

What little there was, even her idle time was filled with some type of adventurous activity. White-water rafting. Water-skiing. Ferris wheels. Roller coasters. There wasn't a roller coaster built that Patricia Blakley wouldn't ride. The higher the better. The more dangerous; the greater the hrill.

Despite her love of adventure, it was a white-picket fence and flower garden and cozy, loved-filled home Patricia longed for the most. A home filled with the patter of children's feet, the smell of baking cookies, and a loving husband to care for.

Now she was about to walk down the aisle. In a few moments, the life she had dreamed of would begin. Patricia took a deep breath and tried to calm her nerves.

CHAPTER FOUR

Driving back to Brandon Station Court, DeBerry thumped out the last Kool from his crumpled pack. He rolled down the window, then punched the volume on the radio. The twang of a banjo and the soft stroke of a fiddle could barely be heard above the static. An accomplished banjo picker himself, if DeBerry couldn't listen to his beloved bluegrass, he wasn't going to listen to anything at all. He turned the radio off and lit his cigarette. "This one's going to get ugly," he said to Church. "I've got that feeling."

Church sighed. "Judging by all the people at the church, she sure had a lot of people that cared about her."

"Yeah, well there was at least one person that didn't care too much about her." He pulled alongside the curb and parked behind one of the fire trucks. Now after midnight, most of the trucks had already left. A few remained to provide support personnel and lighting.

DeBerry and Church stopped in the carport before

entering the house. The ID tech was positioned over the body, taking pictures from different angles. After one final click, he looked at DeBerry and Church. "Ready to turn her over?"

Carefully, they rolled the body onto its back. The right side of the chest was partially burned through, leaving the ribs and chest cavity exposed. Part of the lower abdomen was also open. The skin had split in several places, worst around the scalp, chest, and thighs. Despite the severe charring, a small tuft of brown hair remained near the rear base of the skull.

"Hey, Dee," the sergeant from the Crime Lab called to DeBerry from the kitchen. "Come see what they found in the bedroom."

DeBerry and Church followed the other sergeant into the bedroom.

"I'll be damned," DeBerry said as he examined the Glock .45. One round was missing from an otherwise full magazine. "Can we get prints?"

The sergeant shook his head. "It was underneath a pile of rubble. Been stepped on, watered down, you name it. Even if we could get a lift, it wouldn't be usable."

"Were there any other guns?" Church asked.

"Nope. Just this one."

Church and DeBerry glanced at one another. Then Church asked, "You didn't find any other guns anywhere in the house?"

Again, the sergeant shook his head. "Should there be?"

Church shrugged. "The husband said he kept three guns here in the house."

"Maybe whoever did this took them to make it look

more like a burglary," the sergeant said. "They sure didn't bother to make anything else look real."

Church looked around at the stacked dresser drawers, the mattress neatly pulled halfway off the bed. He didn't buy it. It was the sloppiest staged burglary he had ever seen.

Church left the two sergeants and wandered into one of the other bedrooms.

A rolling Craftsman toolbox, so new the red paint still gleamed, sat askew to the wall as if someone had attempted to move it. Church opened the top drawer and found each tool, spit-shine new, neatly arranged in an arch. It looked like the owner, let alone a burglar, had never even touched the tools.

There was a small desk against the far wall and a two-drawer file cabinet beside it. The desk was as neatly arranged as the toolbox, each pencil lying in perfect order in the center drawer. A 35-millimeter Olympus camera sat near the corner of the desk, untouched.

Money. Tools. A camera. All hot items on a burglar's list. Yet none of them were taken.

Church fingered through the file cabinet. Warranties and other information on appliances were neatly separated by category, each in a separate, labeled folder. Bank statements were filed in chronological order. Some were labeled Patricia G. Blakley. Toward the back, they were labeled Patricia Kimble.

Patricia Blakley. That was it. That was the name of the frightened young woman he had talked with before. Church sighed with a long, slow breath.

He thumbed through one of the statement envelopes and stared at the signature on the canceled checks. Patricia B. Kimble. A beautiful, sweeping signature. Very neat, free flowing. Void of any troubling glitches.

He slipped the envelope into his pocket, then rejoined DeBerry.

It was a little after 4:00 A.M. when Church arrived home. On the way to his bedroom, he looked into his daughter Dana's empty room. Although Dana was twenty-two years old, already married, and in December would graduate with a degree in nursing from the University of North Carolina at Greensboro, Church couldn't get used to her empty bedroom. Part of him looked forward to grandkids, but the other part still wanted her at home. He wanted to know she was safe, protected from the outside world. Still, he knew there was only so much safety and security he could offer.

He quietly closed the door, then peeked in on his son Jeremy. Jeremy was a sophomore at Guilford Technical Community College. Like his father, he had a keen interest in fire service. Already a volunteer fireman at the same station as his father, Jeremy planned to carry his interest one step further and become a paid fireman with one of the stations in Greensboro.

Firemen, cops, doctors, nurses—careers often passed down from one generation to the next. Maybe it was a desire to follow in the father or mother's footsteps. Maybe it was the instilled appreciation of public service that drew children to follow their parents' career paths. Or for many, maybe it was simply the only life they knew.

Whatever the reason, Jim Church ultimately followed his mother. She was a nurse; his father, a furniture maker and farmer.

The youngest of eight, Church went away to college to escape the family farm, only to return to the only life he really knew. Farming wasn't a bad life. It had always provided well for his family. They had everything they ever *needed*—plenty of food, warm clothes. But they never had the money for things they *wanted.*

Church wanted more for Dana and Jeremy. He wanted them to set their sights high and to know that with a little determination, anything was possible.

He used to strap Dana's baby seat onto the back of the tractor while he plowed the fields. At night when his wife Brenda got off work, Church went to class. It took awhile, but eventually Church earned enough credits to graduate from college with degrees in both psychology and criminal justice. At thirty-four, he put both degrees to work and signed on with the Guilford County Sheriff's Department.

Church closed Jeremy's door, then quietly stepped into his and Brenda's bedroom.

Brenda was asleep and barely stirred when Church sat down on the side of the bed. They had been married twenty-five years. Between his work as a cop and a volunteer fireman, she was used to the middle-of-the-night hours.

Church was one of the lucky ones. Brenda seldom complained about the interrupted holidays, missed engagements, or canceled plans. She went about her own business, had reheated more dinners than she could count, and enjoyed the friendships of her coworkers at Moses Cone Hospital. As the wife of a detective, Brenda learned early on to cope with the unpredictable curves her husband's job could throw. She figured you either cope or you don't. She'd seen too many marriages of Church's coworkers end because the wife often couldn't accept the responsibilities and dangers of the job. But for most officers, it wasn't just a *job*. It was *who* they were. When you accepted them, you accepted their way of life.

Church slipped off his shoes. Though bone-tired, he couldn't lie down. He kept replaying in his mind the conversation with Ted Kimble. Was it his imagination, or had Ted shown little emotion? Ted's eyes were bright and clear, without even a hint of red. He appeared more tired than stressed. Had Brenda's life been in question, God only knows how many people it would have taken to calm him. Tired or not.

Church pushed the thoughts aside. He had better get some sleep. Tomorrow would be a nonstop day. He had been the detective on call. It was standard procedure for that detective to be assigned the case.

He had assisted the other Major Crimes detectives, Steve McBride and Herb Byrd, with homicide investigations, and had even assisted DeBerry. But whether it was luck or fate, the roulette wheel had yet to spin Church's number. Until tonight. He had never been on call when a homicide came in. He had never soloed on a homicide.

CHAPTER FIVE

The following morning, Church took the back steps of the Guilford County Sheriff's Department two at a time. He burst through the door on the second floor and hurried to his office.

Church, Steve "Mac" McBride, and Herb Byrd all shared a crowded space. They were just far enough apart that no man sat on another's lap. Yet they were so close, each could smell what the others had eaten for lunch. An equally crowded conference room separated the detectives from DeBerry's office, which, with a few shelves and bar racks, would have made a nice walk-in closet.

While most other officers proudly displayed framed certificates of accomplishment on the walls near their desks, DeBerry's various certificates lay haphazardly in the top drawer of his desk. Only two items decorated his office wall: a polished wooden clock cut into the shape of a guitar and a certificate from the Whilton School of Cake Decorating.

Never one to take the normal route to anything,

DeBerry had taken the class shortly after his divorce. He claimed decorating cakes would give him and his two young daughters something fun to do on the weekends they stayed with him. His daughters were barely old enough to pour a glass of milk, let alone decorate a cake. Many, though, saw through the sly smile. Knowing he avoided bars and other more-traveled routes, they shook their heads and laughed at the interesting possibilities a cake-decorating class could offer the good-looking, single detective. The women in the class, however, were for the most part old enough to be his grandmother. The kind, little old ladies, with their silver hair and bifocals and aged-spotted hands, overlooked the oddity of having a man in their class and took him under their maternal wings. Although his basic idea might not have worked, DeBerry was never one to quit and came away from the class as the Sheriff's Department's official cake decorator.

DeBerry's pranks and jokes and offbeat doings were legendary in the department. Yet he was a loner. He existed in his own world, venturing out only long enough to pull a trademark joke on an unsuspecting colleague. Colleagues often worried, and sometimes feared, what abstract thought would next project itself from DeBerry's deviously brilliant mind.

DeBerry was the kid in school who always tempted suspension. Principals knew his parents on a first-name basis. But it was all good natured, and one couldn't help but like the kid with the off-center smile. He once drove a motorcycle down the main hallway of his high school, parking it in the lobby of the school auditorium. Always punctual, he claimed he didn't want to be late for class. He played football in high school for one of the best teams in the state. He was the football player the cheerleaders' parents worried about. People who knew DeBerry as a kid shook their heads when told he chose law enforcement as a career, but they weren't really surprised. They figured he would end up on one side of a set of bars sooner or later, they just weren't ever sure which side.

Preferring experience to textbooks, DeBerry bypassed college for a stint in the Army, then signed on with the Sheriff's Department when he was only twenty years old. He pulled his duty as a patrol officer until his perceptive mind and natural inquisitiveness led him into investigations. He and a senior officer answered a possible suicide call one night while on patrol. The young deputy became fascinated with the blood spatters he saw. No one could explain to him the difference between the various patterns. So he studied, experimented, and studied some more until he was confident that a victim's cause of death could often be determined by the blood spatters. This fascination fueled his passion for cracking homicide cases.

However, on mornings like this, DeBerry wondered why he couldn't be a professional fisherman. A crowd of reporters jostled for position outside his open door, their pens and notepads poised for information.

"The sheriff will make a press release sometime this morning, folks," he pleaded. "Until then, I can't tell you a thing."

"Is it true she was shot?" one reporter asked.

DeBerry raised his hands. "Folks, I can't tell you

a thing. At this time, we're not even sure the victim *was* a she. We'll know more when we get the autopsy report back." He reached for his empty coffee cup and lifted it in a salute. "Now, if you'll excuse me, I'm going to get a much-needed cup of coffee."

"Was the fire intentionally set?" one of the reporters asked.

"That's still under investigation. The Fire Marshall's office hasn't made a ruling yet."

"Is the sheriff involved in the investigation?"

"The sheriff is involved in *all* of our investigations." DeBerry gave his cockeyed grin and again tempted to escape the cramped office. "We have your fax numbers, and we'll send a statement as soon as the sheriff releases it. Thanks for coming. Y'all have a good day, now." He elbowed his way through the crowd and marched toward the coffeepot. It was empty. He bit his tongue and swallowed the word he wanted to say in fear of seeing it in print.

A persistent reporter had followed DeBerry into the conference room and stood so close, the sergeant backed into him when he turned around. "When will we hear something about the autopsy report?" the reporter asked.

"December." DeBerry stood toe-to-toe with the reporter and looked him squarely in the eyes.

The reporter accepted the information at first, then scowled. "It doesn't take that long to get an autopsy report back."

"No, but it may take me that long to get the information to *you* if you don't move and let me get a cup of coffee."

"Oh." The reporter backed off and half-heartedly nodded.

"We should have it back this afternoon," DeBerry said, his voice falling softer. "We'll fax a release as soon as we can. The sooner we can get to work, the sooner you'll have it." He motioned toward the door and smiled.

As soon as the reporter left, Lieutenant Grady Bryant came in. Bryant oversaw the Special Operations division of the Sheriff's Department, including the Major Crimes Unit. At forty-seven, he was a hard-line, no-nonsense lawman. The law was the law, and it wasn't meant to be broken. He had been with the department twenty-seven years. The lines that landscaped his forehead were cut deep with experience. Both he and DeBerry had come up the ranks the old-fashioned way—through hard work and experience. Unlike the department's recent years, with a 400-person payroll and specialized divisions, he and DeBerry remembered when the department was only 40 strong and patrol officers doubled as investigators. That was back when one relied more on instinct than on a textbook. When respect was earned, not demanded by a rank.

"Where do we stand?" Bryant asked, thrusting his hands deep into the pockets of his khakis. He rocked back and forth on the balls of his feet.

"Herb's on his way to Chapel Hill for the autopsy," DeBerry said. He dumped two scoops of black coffee into a filter and pushed it into the coffeemaker. "Mac's pulled the CRT and a couple of the district detectives to help canvas the neighborhood."

The CRT, or Crime Repression Team, was a specialized division like the Major Crimes Unit. They provided backup for other divisions by assisting in canvases and roadblocks, and also by providing canine support. They were highly trained, and most were members of the sheriff's emergency response team.

"You using the dogs?" Bryant asked.

"Already got them out there."

Bryant nodded. "Sheriff wants you to do a press release as soon as possible. Let him proof it, though, before you send it."

DeBerry grinned. Sure, he'd do a release as soon as he could. It wasn't like he had anything else to do. He sighed and watched with great anticipation as a slow stream of coffee began to drip into the heavily-stained carafe.

While waiting, he stepped into his detectives' office. Church was the only one at his desk, busy transcribing last night's notes.

"You want this case, Jim?" DeBerry asked.

Church looked up at the sergeant. The question had caught him off guard. "Pardon?"

DeBerry sat down on the edge of McBride's desk. "Do you want this case?"

Church leaned back in his chair and stared at DeBerry. "I was the detective on call. I thought it was standard procedure."

The sergeant nodded slightly then pursed his lips. He sighed, then said, "Normally, it *is* procedure. But you've never handled a homicide by yourself, Jim. Especially one of this nature."

Church slowly drummed a pen against the edge of his desk.

"Look," DeBerry said, his voice softening. "I'm not questioning anyone's ability. I have just as much confidence in you as I do in Mac or Herb. All I'm saying is, this one has the potential to get real ugly. If you want it, you've got it. If not, I'll assign it to Herb or Mac. It's your call."

Church shook his head. "No. I want it."

DeBerry stood. "Then you've got it."

Church started with Patricia's brother and his wife, Reuben and Kristy Blakley. He gunned the Lumina and headed out of Greensboro toward the new Highway 220 bypass.

Reuben and Kristy lived in Deerfield South, a newer subdivision across the Randolph County line, just south of Guilford County. The houses were a mixture of Cape Cod, ranch-style, and cottage-like bungalows, each on an acre lot. The residents were far enough away from the hustle of the city, yet still close enough to borrow a cup of sugar from the neighbors. The front yards were well manicured with carpets of lush, thick grass. Some of the back yards sported swing sets and bicycles and other tell-all evidence of children nearby.

Church found their house and pulled into the driveway. Kristy met him at the front door. Although she was dressed for a new day in a soft print dress, her tired eyes couldn't hide the fact, that for her, the previous night had yet to end. Her auburn hair was cut short and pushed behind her ears. The ends flipped forward, framing her delicate face. Church had spoken to her only briefly the night before at the church and guessed her to be in her mid-twenties, although both she and Reuben seemed mature beyond their years.

"Reuben will be out in a moment," Kristy said as she ushered Church into the living room. "Can I get you something to drink?"

"No, I'm fine, thank you."

The room was bright and open, comfortable. The country-style decorations were tasteful and conservative in nature. A Bible lay open on one of the end tables.

Kristy showed Church to the sofa, then sank into the comfort of the matching loveseat. "We finally got Sheila to bed around six this morning," she said.

"Sheila—Patricia's mother?" Church asked.

"Oh, yes. I'm sorry. She stayed with us last night. Reuben didn't want her to be alone." She looked at Church for a moment, then added, "Sheila and Reuben's father, Richard, are divorced. Grandma Blakley lives with Richard, but Sheila lives by herself. We just didn't want her to have to . . . you know, be alone."

Church understood and nodded.

Reuben came down the hallway and sat down beside his wife on the loveseat. He was a young man with huge blue eyes and a sand-colored crewcut. "When will we know for sure if it was Patricia?" he asked directly.

"We should have the reports back later today." Church leaned forward on the sofa, propping his arms on his knees. "Why don't you start from the beginning, Reuben, and tell me what happened."

Reuben draped his arm around Kristy's shoulder and settled into the soft cushions. "I had worked all day yesterday with Daddy in Raleigh. We had just gotten home about eight o'clock last night, and I jumped in the shower. Kristy brought me the phone and said that it was Ted. I knew something must be up if he couldn't wait until I got out of the shower to talk.

"He said that he had been trying to reach Patricia and couldn't get her to answer the phone, so he asked if we'd ride over there and make sure everything was okay. I asked him if he had tried the church, and he said he couldn't get an answer there, either."

"Was that at South Elm Street Baptist?"

Reuben nodded. "Yes."

"Is Patricia a member there?"

"We all are. Well, except Ted's family. Mr. Kimble's the pastor at Monnett Road Baptist Church."

"That's Ted's father?"

Reuben nodded.

"Was he there at South Elm Street last night?"

"No, he was out of town. He's on his way back now, though. Everyone's supposed to meet over here in a little while."

"Why didn't Ted go down to the house himself?"

"He was at work and couldn't get off. He couldn't keep running to use the phone, either."

"Where does he work?"

"Well, he was at Precision Fabrics last night. It's a second job. He normally works at Lyles' Building Supplies. Well, he don't just *work* there—he owns it."

"Lyles' Building Supplies?"

Reuben nodded.

Church was familiar with the company, although he had never shopped there. Located in Greensboro on West Lee Street, it was one of the smaller home-building material stores to survive the influx of larger chain stores. It catered more to the do-it-yourselfer than the contractors.

"What does Ted do at Precision Fabrics?" Church asked.

Reuben shrugged and looked at Kristy. "I'm not sure. I think he just works on the production line."

"How long has he been there?"

Again, he turned to his wife. "I don't know, maybe a few weeks. He just started."

"It's been about a month," Kristy added.

"Why did he take a second job? Is the building supply store not doing well financially?"

The young couple looked at one another as if there was no sure answer. "I don't think the company was as strong as it was before Ted bought it," Reuben answered. "But I can't really say for sure."

Church pondered the question himself. "Okay, let's go back to the phone call."

"I was really tired and didn't feel like going over there, but . . . there was something in Ted's voice. He was . . . well, he was almost in a panic. So we hung up, and I thought before I rode over there, I'd try to get her on the phone myself. She never answered, and when the answering machine didn't pick up, I started getting worried. I guess with the panic in Ted's voice, and then when I couldn't get her either, I got a little scared."

"So you left here and drove over to Patricia's house?"

"Yes."

"What time was this?"

"Around eight-thirty, I guess. When we got there, Patricia's car was in the driveway, and I could see smoke coming out of the vents of the house." Reuben looked away. He gazed at the Bible on the end table.

Kristy pulled a tissue from an open box and dabbed at her eyes.

Reuben continued. "I ran to the back door and felt it and could tell it was hot. I told Kristy to check the front door. It was hot, too. Then I started running to each of the windows to see if maybe I could see her inside, but . . . there was so much smoke. We tried to call 911, but we were on a cell phone, and the signal wouldn't go through. I told Kristy to go get Daddy, and I'd keep trying 911."

"Richard lives right down the road from Patricia," Kristy said. She nervously twisted the tissue into a tiny ball. "It's not even two miles."

"After Kristy left," Reuben continued, "I ran up the road to a clearing and was finally able to get a call out. The fire department got there right after Daddy and Kristy got back." He squeezed Kristy's shoulder and took a deep breath. "Once they got there, we just sort of stood back and let them do their jobs."

Kristy lifted her glasses and wiped away the tears. She reached for Reuben's hand. "Detective Church," she said, her voice almost as small as she was, "why is the Sheriff's Department involved in this? I mean, you don't think . . ."

"Anytime there's a body found in this situation, we have to look at it from all angles. We certainly hope it's not the case here, but we have to rule out certain possibilities."

Reuben and Kristy looked at one another, each squeezing the other's hand.

"Reuben," Church asked, "do you know anyone

who might have wanted to harm your sister?"

Again, they turned to one another. Reuben started to speak, then stopped. He swallowed hard, confusion distorting his boyish face. Finally, in a painfully soft voice, he muttered, "Maybe."

CHAPTER SIX

Around four o'clock that afternoon, Church stood in the carport at Patricia and Ted's house with DeBerry, Lt. Bryant, and Sheriff B.J. Barnes. They were waiting for Patricia's family to arrive. Detective Herb Byrd had returned to Greensboro with the autopsy report earlier that afternoon. Church had asked the Blakleys and Kimbles to meet them at the scene. Barnes had scheduled a press conference for the five o'clock newscasts to announce the results of the autopsy. And to ask for the public's help.

Barnes was in the first year of his first term in office. Young by most standards, he was as well respected and liked by his own department as he was by the voting public. He was a massive man, standing nearly six feet seven inches, broad-shouldered and barrel-chested. He carried his weight well. Whether it was his size or his respectability, few saw the need to argue with him.

A former vice cop, Barnes had spent years in the dirt-filled trenches with tough-talking lowlifes. Now, he spent time with smooth-talking politicians. He had made the transition well without having to wear a coat of false airs. Barnes was genuine, no matter whose hand he was shaking.

The news crews had already begun setting up. Their vans, with colorful logos and towering satellite receivers, jammed the dead-end street. Engineers surveyed the thick tree line, worrying if their signals would transmit while the reporters tempted the crime scene tape.

Investigators scoured the front and back yards, the house, the surrounding woods. Canine officers and their four-legged Belgian Malinois partners carefully roamed the area while fire investigators sifted through the rubble.

The Blakleys and Kimbles arrived in a small caravan and pulled to the curb. Bewildered, they stared at the mass of news media. Church's throat knotted as he watched them approach. He hated this part.

Church introduced the families to the sheriff, then turned to Ted. "I need to speak with you for a moment in private, Ted."

Ted looked at his mother, then scanned the grim faces of the detectives. He swallowed hard. "Sure," he said, his voice barely above a whisper. He followed Church to the gazebo.

Church collected his thoughts, then spoke calmly and clearly. "Ted, the body we found in the house was your wife. It *was* Patricia."

Ted rested his hands on his hips and stared at the ground. "Well, I already know that." He glanced up at Church, then stared at the canines sniffing around the edge of the woods.

Church took a deep breath to conceal his shock at Ted's less than emotional reaction. After a moment, he continued. "Ted, the autopsy report showed something else. Your wife didn't die in the fire."

Ted's gaze darted in Church's direction. Then, again, he looked away.

"Ted, your wife died from a single gunshot wound to the head."

At that, Sheila Blakley collapsed to the ground. She had been standing only a few feet away when she overheard the fate of her daughter. She was a tiny woman, but the wail that came from her was primal. Taken aback, Church locked eyes with the woman. The wrenching pain she was suffering shattered his heart. It took him a moment to bring himself back to the conversation with Ted.

"She probably walked in on a burglary," Ted said. He watched his mother-in-law for a moment, then returned his attention to the dogs. "We've been broken into a couple of times."

Church pulled his attention away from the sobbing woman and stared at Ted. "You said you had three guns in the house. We've only been able to find one. Why don't we go in the house and you can show me where you kept them." He lightly touched Ted's elbow and started to step toward the house, but Ted jerked his arm away.

"I said I only had one in the house. I keep the other at the office."

Church stared at him. "Ted, you told me and Sergeant DeBerry last night at the church that you had three here in the house."

"The Remington's at the office."

"What about the Win-Mag? Where is it?"

"I never said I had a Win-Mag."

Church lifted his hand, searching for clarification. "Wait a minute, Ted. You told me and the sergeant that you owned a Glock .45, a Remington, and a 300 Winchester Magnum."

"I didn't say I owned the Win-Mag yet. I said I was thinking about buying one."

Church sorted it out in his head. Maybe he had misunderstood. "Okay, then, what about the Glock. Was it loaded?"

Ted nodded. "Oh, yeah. I always keep it loaded and ready. With a full mag and one in the chamber."

CHAPTER SEVEN

Later that evening, DeBerry sank into Byrd's chair and propped his feet on the desk.

He stared at the collage of photos Byrd had tacked up on the wall behind his desk. Photos of kids, grandkids, and Byrd's classic Camaro he had rebuilt. Entangled in the pictures were love notes written by the hand of a child to "grandpa" and pages of elementary writing exercises, each letter of the alphabet, uppercase and lowercase, carefully crafted on wide, blue-lined paper.

Herb Byrd was a big man with an even bigger heart. He was a damn good investigator, too.

DeBerry turned away from the reminders of happy marriages and ideal family lives. "You had dinner?" he asked Church.

Church shook his head and continued typing his notes into the computer. "I don't think I ever had lunch."

DeBerry yawned. "Damn, if this ol' body ain't tired." He freed himself from his tie and wondered what masochist invented the damn things. "So, Kimble said he thought she walked in on a burglary?"

"Yeah, and that's a bunch of bull. You don't know how many hours I spent with that girl going over safety measures after the first burglary. She would have never stepped foot in that house if she thought something wasn't right."

"What about the pry marks on the front door?"

"They're old. Been there since the last burglary. The only forced entry was the firemen's, when they busted the window."

"What about the back door?"

Church shook his head. "Alan Fields said it wasn't even locked. Opened right up." He stared at the computer screen. He was a detective, not a typist. He retyped a sentence he had accidentally deleted. "Didn't Ted tell us he had three guns in the house?"

"Yep. A Glock, a Remington, and a Win-Mag."

"He's saying now that he told us he keeps the Remington at the office and doesn't even own a Win-Mag. He wants to buy one, though."

DeBerry laughed. "Is that suppose to count? If it is, I want a yacht." He stood and pressed his hands deep into his lower back. "I'm going home to get some sleep. I suggest you do the same."

"That an order?" Church asked.

DeBerry yawned again. "If you want it to be. I'm outta here. Catch you in the morning."

"Night." Church looked at his watch. It was a little past nine. He called Brenda.

"You okay?" she asked.

"Yeah, just a little tired. I'm going to finish this report, then I'll be on home."

"Call me before you leave and I'll heat up your dinner."

"What am I having?" he asked.

"Country-style steak."

"Sounds good. I'll see you in a little bit." He hung up, then dialed the voice mail system. He had checked only three messages when one caught his full attention.

It was the staff duty officer reciting the phone number of someone who had called in on the Crimestoppers line. Someone concerned about the murder of Patricia Kimble.

Church replayed the message and scribbled down the number. All Church knew was that the caller was female. She wouldn't leave her name. He pressed the button until he got a dial tone and quickly dialed the number.

A woman answered.

"This is Detective Jim Church with the Guilford County Sheriff's Department. I'm calling in regards to Patricia Kimble."

There was a slight gasp on the other end of the line. Then the woman spoke. "I'm sorry, Detective who? I didn't catch your name."

"Detective Church. And who am I speaking with?" Church flipped to a fresh page in his notebook and poised his pen.

There was hesitation on the other end of the line. "That's not important right now. I'm a friend of Patricia's." The woman's voice broke as she began to cry.

"I was told by the staff duty officer you may have

information about Patricia's death. Can I meet you somewhere?"

"No! I don't want anyone to know I've called. *Anyone*!" Her voice was racked with sobs. "I'm scared. If he did this to his own . . . *please*, just listen to me. I don't want to give my name."

"All right, it's okay. You don't have to." Church spoke slowly and reassuringly. "You said if *he* did this—who is *he*? Who are you talking about?"

The woman corralled her composure and took a deep breath. "Ted."

Church stared at his notebook. Subconsciously, before the woman had said a name, he had written the letter "T."

"What makes you think Ted was involved in his wife's death?"

"Ted's not the man people think he is. It's all just a charade. Patricia was scared . . . she knew . . ." The woman began to cry again.

"Patricia knew what? What was she scared of?"

"She was scared of Ted. Of what he would do. What he was planning."

"What do you mean? Was Ted violent? Did he abuse Patricia?"

"No," she sobbed, "it wasn't like that. They were having . . . problems. It was like Ted didn't want to be married anymore."

"How do you know this?"

"Patricia told me. We were best friends." She choked back tears that eclipsed her words and continued. "Patricia and I were really close. She confided in me. She told me that she didn't think Ted wanted to spend any time alone with her. They did things together, but they were never alone."

"So you think Ted may have had something to do with his wife's murder because he didn't want to be alone with her anymore?"

"No, that's not all of it. They were having money problems, too. I don't mean they were seriously in debt or anything like that, but Patricia's always been real careful with her money. She told me Ted was spending it as fast as they could make it."

"Is that why he took a second job?"

"No. Patricia thought it was just another excuse to be away from her."

"But wouldn't a second job have helped them with the money situation?"

"You don't understand—they didn't *need* the money. Their bills were being paid with their regular jobs but Ted just kept wanting more. Like he wanted this motorcycle, but Patricia told him they couldn't afford it right then. He got really mad."

Church was trying to see the larger picture. But he couldn't fault a man for taking a second job to pay for something he wanted. He had taken plenty of off-duty uniform assignments to earn a little extra cash.

"And then last week, Patricia told me about the life insurance."

Her words shoved aside any thoughts of second jobs or hard-working men. "What about the life insurance?"

"She was so scared. She knew . . ." The woman again began to cry.

This time Church didn't wait for her tears to lessen.

He pushed harder. "She knew what? Tell me what Patricia knew."

"A few weeks ago, they had this big argument over some life insurance. They had plenty, they were both already covered through work, but Ted wanted to take out another policy. Patricia told him they didn't need it. But then she found out . . ." She took a deep breath, teetering on the edge of breaking down again.

"Patricia found out *what*?" Church pushed.

"She found out that Ted had taken it out anyway. He took the policy out without her knowing."

"Was the policy for just Ted himself?"

"No, it was for both of them. Patricia, too. She only found out about it when the doctor's office called to set up her blood work."

"But wouldn't Patricia have had to sign the application if her name was on it?"

"You don't understand. He forged it. Ted forged Patricia's name."

CHAPTER EIGHT

DeBerry longed for a quiet, lazy morning when he could actually finish a cup of coffee. This wasn't to be the morning.

"What's this about the insurance?" Lt. Bryant asked as he followed DeBerry into his office.

"According to a friend of Patricia's, Ted forged her name on a life insurance application. Church is on the phone now with the agent to see if we can't get a copy of it." DeBerry took off his coat and hung it on the brass tree outside his office. He unbuttoned the sleeves of his starched shirt and rolled them to his elbows. He hated starch. "Church called me last night at home after he talked with her."

"Did she call in here?"

"Through Crimestoppers." DeBerry plopped into his soft leather chair, one he had confiscated from a retiring major, and glanced at the guitar clock. It was 7:55. He couldn't remember if he had slept the night before. "Jerry Webster's going to meet us at the scene at 10:00," he told Bryant. "I'm going to have him reconstruct the fire and see if we can't get close on a time of death."

Jerry Webster was an arson specialist with the State Bureau of Investigation. The SBI worked as a support unit to other law enforcement agencies across North Carolina. They were sometimes called in to assist when their vast technical knowledge or access to varied records was needed.

Church joined DeBerry and Bryant in the sergeant's office. "Robert Gerald will be here in about thirty minutes. He's the insurance agent," Church said.

DeBerry nodded. "Good. That'll still give us time to meet Webster."

McBride poked his head into the crowded office. He was the youngest of the Major Crimes detectives and had come into the unit after making a name for himself as a damn good juvenile investigator. Still in his thirties, McBride hadn't yet begun to worry about a middle-aged paunch. After all, he had mastered the martial arts more as a way to relax than for its physical benefits. "Got anything you want me to do?" he asked.

"Yeah," DeBerry answered. "How about going over to Precision Fabrics and checking out Kimble's alibi. If he took a piss break, we want to know about it."

McBride mock-saluted and left.

"Oh," Bryant said as he, too, turned to leave. "You know the little girl over in Records? They're having a baby shower for her and asked if you'd do the cake."

DeBerry shook his head. "I don't do baby shower

or wedding cakes. Now, I can do a damn good Bugs Bunny if she wants Bugs."

Bryant grinned. "I don't think Bugs is what they had in mind."

Back at his desk, Church pulled the file on the second burglary at the Kimble's house. Since Church hadn't worked the case, he wasn't familiar with it. It had happened just over a year ago. Shortly afterwards, a man named Howard Sawyer had been arrested. As he scanned the list of stolen items, one caught his attention: an Olympus 35-millimeter camera.

Hadn't the camera sitting on the desk in the second bedroom been an Olympus?

Church bet that unless the Kimbles had bought the same type of camera after the burglary, it was the same one. It had never been stolen.

But why would Patricia have falsified a report? It certainly didn't fit her character.

Church flipped pages until he found the bottom of the report. Ted, not Patricia, had signed it.

Church typed the case number into the computer to see if it had yet gone to trial. Sure enough, Howard Sawyer had recently been convicted and was being held in the county jail waiting transfer.

Church grabbed the list of stolen items and tore out of the office, racing down the hall to the jail.

A few minutes later, Howard Sawyer entered the interview room where Church was waiting. The faded orange jumpsuit Sawyer wore stretched against his bulk. His sandals popped against his thick feet with each step. His left biceps bore a tattoo of an eagle.

Church extended his hand. "Mr. Sawyer, Detective Church."

Sawyer accepted the proffered hand, then took a seat at the small table.

"So, you're awaiting transfer?" Church asked, seated across from Sawyer.

"So they tell me."

Church figured that was enough of the pleasantries. Besides, he didn't have much time. He wasn't altogether sure he could trust the word of a convicted felon, but at this point, what did Sawyer have to lose?

"You were convicted of a burglary at 2104 Brandon Station Court. I want you to take a look at this list of items reported stolen and see if they match the items you were charged with stealing."

Sawyer raised his pudgy hands. "Hey, man, I've already been tried on those charges."

"This doesn't have anything to do with you, Mr. Sawyer. It's an entirely different case."

"Then what do you need with me?"

"There was a homicide at this residence earlier—"

"Whoa! Back up, Detective." The metal legs of the chair squealed against the worn tile as Sawyer pushed away from the table. "I ain't involved in no homicide."

Church slowly looked around the room. "Well, unless you're Casper the Friendly Ghost and can fly through walls, I'd say you have an airtight alibi, wouldn't you, Mr. Sawyer?" Church slid the list across the desk and turned it so Sawyer could read it.

"I'm just asking for your help, Mr. Sawyer. That's all. You have nothing to lose."

Sawyer studied Church for a moment, then looked down at the list. He crinkled his pug nose and smirked.

"What about the camera?" Church asked. "Did you take a camera?"

Sawyer shook his head. "I didn't take half this shit."

"What about the jewelry?"

Again, Sawyer shook his head. "There was a necklace there, if I remember right. But I didn't take it. It was cheap shit. I wouldn't have gotten a dollar for it."

Church scanned over the report until he found the necklace. It was reported as a twenty-four-carat gold herringbone chain valued at $600.

"Mr. Sawyer, I do thank you," Church said as he stood. "And good luck with the transfer."

"Hope you catch the guy. Killing someone ain't right."

"Oh, we'll get him. Sooner or later, we usually get our man."

"Yeah, I know." Sawyer smiled. He was missing a front tooth.

As Church hurried back down the hall, he noticed a heavyset man sitting on the cushioned bench outside the secretary's area. The man was sweating profusely and dabbed nervously at his brow with a handkerchief. He held a briefcase tight to his chest as his gaze darted up and down the hall.

That's got to be the insurance agent, Church thought. The man had been so nervous on the telephone he could barely speak. "Mr. Gerald?" Church asked as he approached the man.

"Yes, yes. I'm Robert Gerald. Are you Detective Church?" Gerald stood and nearly dropped the briefcase. He scrambled to hold onto it and the handkerchief.

"Yes, I'm Church." The detective offered his hand, then awkwardly let it drop. It was hopeless to try to shake the man's trembling hand. "Glad you could come on such short notice. Why don't you come on back here to my sergeant's office and we can talk there."

"Certainly. I brought all the paperwork—the application and a copy of the policy as it would have been written on Mrs. Kimble. I had an uneasy feeling about that boy."

Gerald continued his nervous chatter as he followed Church down the hallway and into DeBerry's office. DeBerry looked up from a stack of new cases he was assigning and motioned them in. "Come on in and have a seat. Jim, just move those folders to the corner over there."

Church introduced the men, then cleared the stack of folders from one of the chairs.

"Can we get you a cup of coffee, or a soda maybe?" DeBerry asked Gerald.

"No, no, I'm fine. Thank you." Gerald dabbed at his brow with the dampened cloth. "I knew something wasn't right with this application. Mrs. Kimble was so upset about it."

DeBerry relaxed and leaned back in his chair, hoping his relaxed state would help calm the poor man. "When you say she was upset, was she angry?"

"She was more . . . *distressed*, maybe? Oh, she was a bit angry, too, I could tell. But she was such a nice young lady, I think she tried to hide it. You know what I mean?"

DeBerry nodded. "Sort of out of her character, maybe?"

"Yes, yes, exactly. She didn't want to cause a scene." Gerald opened his briefcase, removed the application, and handed it to Church.

Church stared at the signature. It definitely wasn't the same signature as those on the canceled checks he had seen earlier. "A hundred thousand dollars," he said, handing the application to DeBerry.

"Yes, but there's a rider." Gerald leaned forward and pointed to the last paragraph. "In case of accidental death, it pays *two* hundred thousand."

DeBerry examined it for a moment, then handed it back to Church. "When did you first meet Ted Kimble, Mr. Gerald?"

"A few weeks ago. He called and said he and his wife were interested in a life insurance policy. I met with him a few times and showed him some figures."

"Was Mrs. Kimble at any of these meetings?"

Gerald shook his head. His caterpillar-like mustache twitched. "No, as a matter of fact, I thought that rather odd."

"Did you ask Ted about it?" Church asked.

"Yes, as a matter of fact I did. He said that he handled all the business affairs and there was no need to involve her. When I told him that she would have to sign the application, he seemed a little bothered."

"Did you go out to their home to meet with him?" Church asked.

"No, I offered. But Mr. Kimble always insisted on meeting at his work."

"That would be Lyles' Building Supplies?" DeBerry asked.

"Yes."

"Were you at Lyles' the day Patricia became so upset?"

"Yes, I never met Mr. Kimble anywhere else. On that day, though, I don't think Mr. Kimble was expecting her. She dropped in, I think, to bring him lunch." He twisted the handkerchief into a knotted rope and blotted his forehead.

"What happened after Patricia arrived?" Church asked.

"Well, she was visibly upset. She started crying and stormed out of the office. I asked Mr. Kimble if I should come back at another time."

"What did he say?"

"He told me no, that she was just under a lot of stress at work. He apologized for her and said he would handle it."

"What happened next?" DeBerry asked.

"I proceeded with the application, but in order for it to be approved, the company requires the applicant to have a medical examination. I called Mrs. Kimble at home to arrange an appointment and she became . . . well, nearly hysterical. She even slammed the phone down."

"Did you tell Ted that you couldn't process the application without the medical exam?"

"This all happened just a few days ago. I tried to

get in touch with him to tell him. But he called me this morning, right after you did, Detective Church."

"Ted called you this morning? What did he want?"

"Well, he said he was trying to arrange the funeral and . . . well, basically, he wanted to know when he could collect."

CHAPTER NINE

Well, I think how last Christmas was—when Mommy left Daddy and I think of all the ways I've grown since then, spiritually. God has really blessed me. I was worried about Mommy but I can tell she's doing a lot better. Christmas was not as bad for her as I thought it would be. Ted spent Christmas Eve and Christmas day with us. I know he's an answer to a prayer, but I'm not sure which one yet.

Patricia Kimble's journal
December 25, 1991

Two days after her daughter's death, Sheila Blakley gripped her son Reuben's arm tightly to steady herself as they entered Hanes-Lineberry Funeral Home. Richard, Kristy, and Bertha followed them in. Sheila had refused to take the Valium the doctor had prescribed, fearing sleep and the nightmares it would bring. Besides, she wanted to be fully alert when they told her that Patricia, her daughter, her best friend, would soon be home.

Sheila had always been painfully shy, preferring to blend her petite, five-foot frame into a nearby corner. Now, she wanted to meld into the shadow of her son. She was disgusted with herself for having to lean on anyone, especially Reuben. He was going through his own grief right now. So was Kristy.

Kristy and Patricia had grown to be more like sisters than sisters-in-law. A bond had formed that went much deeper than the marriage of a sibling implied. Kristy, too, needed Reuben's strength.

But Sheila and Richard could barely carry on a conversation without it erupting into a barrage of bitter words. Sheila kept reminding herself that he, too, had lost a daughter and was feeling the same shock, the same disbelief. But he had his mother, Bertha. Sheila had no one, except Reuben. She prayed Kristy would understand.

"Mrs. Blakley," the well-suited funeral director said as he greeted them at the door. "The Kimbles are waiting downstairs. Is there anyone else we should wait on?"

"No," Reuben said. "We're all here."

The director smiled a soft, understanding smile. "Then we'll go on downstairs."

No one spoke as they followed him down a spiral staircase and into one of the planning rooms.

Sheila's chest tightened as they entered the room. The rich oak paneled walls and lovely framed words of solace did little to lessen her pain. This can't be happening, she thought. It just can't be real. Not Patricia. Not my precious Patricia.

For nine months, she had carried Patricia in her womb. The embryo of her daughter, though, was attached by something much greater and longer lasting than an umbilical cord. Her daughter wasn't just a part of Sheila's body. She was a part of her soul.

"Here, Mrs. Blakley," Ronnie Kimble said, jumping up from one of the upholstered wingback chairs. "You can have my seat."

At twenty-three, two years younger than his brother Ted, Ronnie Kimble was a polite boy, friendly and always well mannered. Although they both stood six feet tall, Ronnie was much leaner, more chiseled than his brother, a result no doubt of his service in the U.S. Marine Corps. His nearly coal-black hair was in a crew cut, and his eyes were nearly as blue as the Marine's dress uniform he wore.

The funeral director left the room and returned a moment later with metal folding chairs tucked under each arm. "These aren't as comfortable as the others, but we certainly don't want anyone to have to stand."

"Oh, I don't mind standing," Ronnie said. "I'm a Marine."

The director looked at him oddly and slightly smiled, then sat in one of the chairs himself and opened a leather portfolio.

Ted, sitting in one of the wingback chairs, nervously tapped his foot. He gnawed hungrily on a ragged cuticle. His father and his mother, Ron and Edna Kimble, sat on the sofa, the reverend's arm draped loosely around his stoic wife's shoulder.

After removing a gold pen from his suit pocket, the

director asked, "Did Patricia have any wishes regarding—"

"First," Ted interrupted, "I don't care how much it's going to cost. Money's not important. I want her to have the best."

The director stared at Ted for a second, then looked back down at his clipboard. "Certainly."

"I want her to h—have a . . . nice casket," Richard stuttered, his lips trembling, his eyes filling with tears.

"Oh, we won't need a casket," Ted said. "She's going to be cremated."

"What?" Richard and Reuben said at the same time, neither believing what they had just heard.

"She's going to be cremated. It's what she wanted."

Richard and Reuben looked at one another. "Since when?" Reuben asked.

"Well, I mean, really—what's the point in a casket? She was practically already cremated in the fire."

Sheila burst into tears.

CHAPTER TEN

Lord, help me to be obedient to you in even the small things as well as the big things. I claim your promise tonight that you will meet all my needs—financially, spiritually, emotionally, and eternally. I claim your promise for the perfect husband that will love me as much as I love him and will accept that I am only perfect in God's eyes through forgiveness. Thank you Lord for your promises!

Patricia Kimble's journal
November 1, 1992

Thanksgiving 1992

Patricia alternated the brown napkins with the orange ones and placed them on the table. She was so excited! She had cooked for Ted before, quite often, but Thanksgiving dinner was special. She wanted everything to be perfect.

They wouldn't be alone. She had invited her mother, Reuben, and Kristy, and Bryan, a friend from church. She felt so sorry for Bryan. Since his breakup with Mandy, he had been so lonely. Lord knows, I know lonely, she thought. She hated for anyone to feel alone, especially having felt so herself for so many years. She prayed daily for the Lord to give her guidance, to let her make a difference in Bryan's life. Everyone needed a good friend.

She wedged two long, vanilla-scented candles in crystal holders and placed them on either side of the floral centerpiece. She fussed at herself for having spent so much money on expensive decorations when simple ones would have done. But then she laughed. Once in a while, she guessed, extravagance wouldn't hurt.

The pleasant aroma of a baking turkey wafted from the oven, reminding her of the Thanksgiving dinners her mother had cooked when Patricia was a child. It was the same every year—Mommy and Grandma, buried up to their elbows in flour and gravies and goodies, Patricia stirring the contents of the bowls, and little Reuben underfoot crying because he wanted to help. When Mommy and Grandma weren't looking, Patricia would let him lick the spoon. It didn't matter what was on it. He just wanted to be a part of the festivities. She would wipe his tears with the corner of the little checked apron Grandma had made her and ask him if the stuffing needed more salt.

Like he really knew, Patricia thought and laughed out loud.

Patricia looked at her gold watch. It was almost

noon. Two more hours and her house would be filled with the kind of joy that makes a house a home. She thanked the Lord for all that was good in her life. She thanked Him for Ted.

CHAPTER ELEVEN

Church stood alone among the rubble of the house and lightly kicked at a piece of charred carpet. The SBI and Fire Marshall's office had determined through a computer re-creation that the fire had burned at least two hours, probably more. Three? Four? Possibly.

He stepped over scattered clumps of Sheetrock and insulation and walked into the hallway. Sunlight filtered through the outside vents into the crawl space, illuminating the black hole where Patricia's body had been found. The medical examiner's report showed her body had contained less than 5 percent carbon monoxide saturation. Patricia was dead long before her body burned.

Her body had been found face down, arms pointing toward the master bedroom. The bullet had entered her brain just behind her left ear and traveled through the left temporal lobe, brain stem, and right temporal lobe. Death occurred instantly, dropping her where she had stood.

At least she felt no pain, Church thought. Unless you consider the emotional pain of perhaps knowing her attacker.

He backed away from the hole, stepping carefully back into the kitchen. Then, slowly, he retraced his steps. Teetering on the edge of the blackened pit, he looked to his left, the direction from which the bullet would have come. He was looking directly into the guest bathroom.

No, Patricia never saw her killer. Whoever it was lay in wait like a coward.

Although Patricia had stood five feet seven, she had a slight frame, barely over a hundred pounds. Why, then, would someone wait in ambush when the killer could have, in all probability, easily overpowered her?

But Patricia wasn't overpowered because she never had a chance to react. She was killed moments, maybe even seconds, after entering the house. She had entered through the back door, walked through the kitchen and into the hallway, heading toward the master bedroom. She would have let the little dog out of the master bathroom, perhaps then changed clothes. But she never made it that far. The little dog died, trapped in the smoking hellhole. Its mistress died right there in the hallway where Church now stood.

Church stared into the hole for a moment, then walked outside. The sun had topped the tree line, spreading its warmth and light to the secluded area. Although thick woods blocked the area, there was nowhere for a car to park and be concealed. If her killer was already inside the house when Patricia arrived, she probably would have seen a car.

He strolled up the driveway to the front of the carport. Patricia's car had been parked in the driveway on the far left side, directly in front of a slight slope of concrete, a ramp used to remove the riding mower. Church stared at the mower parked in the corner of the carport and knew it hadn't been moved recently. Cobwebs stretched from it to the carport wall.

According to Ted, and Patricia's coworkers at Cinnamon Ridge Apartments, Patricia had left work early to mow the yard. Why then did she park directly in front of the area she would have used to drive the mower? Because a car was already parked on the right side of the driveway. And if another car was parked in her driveway, why did she enter the house?

Because she recognized the car. And knew its driver.

She had left her office at 3:30. It would have taken her about fifteen minutes to get home. If she had arrived home by 4:00, she still would have had time to mow the yard, shower, and change clothes for her 7:00 prayer meeting.

But she never made it to the prayer meeting. By 7:00, it was very likely Patricia Kimble had been dead close to three hours.

A slight breeze rustled the leaves and chilled the air despite the glaring sun. The leaves, already showing their fall colors, had turned upward, indicating rain was on the way. The deep red and rusty gold landscape reminded Church of the small mountain town he had grown up in, not unlike Pleasant Garden.

Church pulled into Marion's Corner Mart on the way back to his office in Greensboro. Three older men sat outside on a parson's bench near the door. The conversation, as Church suspected, centered upon the murder.

"Had to have been a stranger," one of the men said.

"Lois had me lock the doors last night," another one said. "First time that door's ever been locked, I guess."

"Guess you better go see Fred and have some keys made."

The men laughed uneasily and politely nodded to Church as he entered the store. Inside, another small group of men gathered around a coffeepot. Again, the conversation was about the murder.

Church listened as he fished a Mountain Dew from the drink cooler. It's normal, he thought, for people to praise the dead. Normal for them to perhaps raise a person's worthiness a notch or two in light of the circumstances. But there was something so genuine in these people's comments. The way they felt about Patricia came from the depths of their hearts. It wasn't simply an emotional reaction to their loss.

Church left Pleasant Garden and headed back to Greensboro.

Back at the office, Church had just sat down at his desk when Sheriff Barnes entered.

Barnes sat down across from him. "Anything new?" the sheriff asked, his voice as strong and powerful as his presence.

"Got a call this morning from the owner of the apartment complex where Patricia worked," Church answered. He sat aside his Burger King lunch and leaned back in his chair. "He said Ted had called him yesterday asking when he could collect from Patricia's life insurance policy with the company."

"This is a different policy than he had already called on?"

Church nodded. "Yeah, he must have called Robert Gerald and this guy the same day. This guy, the owner of the apartments, thought it was pretty odd, too, that he'd be calling to collect only two days after his wife's death."

DeBerry walked in and tossed a file on McBride's desk. He stopped and listened to the conversation.

"What about Kimble's alibi?" Barnes asked.

"Checks out," Church answered. "We've figured the time of death to be between 4:00 P.M. and 6:00 P.M. According to one of the guys that works out at Lyles', a Charles Oliver, Kimble was there all afternoon. Then he clocked in at Precision Fabrics at 6:10."

Barnes absorbed the information. "Is Oliver reliable?"

Church shrugged. "Herb's checking him out."

"Did he sign in at Precision Fabrics, or is it a punch time card?"

"Punch card."

Barnes sighed and stood. "So he's got an alibi."

"I'm thinking accomplice," Church said.

"Could be," DeBerry piped in. "It's a pretty good theory, *if* we can prove it."

Barnes looked at the sergeant and nodded. "Any other suspects?"

"Herb and Mac's chasing down some names, but so far, nothing concrete."

"You know what bugs me about his alibi?" Church asked. "Why would someone who owns a business take a second-shift job that pays six dollars an hour?"

"How long has he been at Precision?" Barnes asked.

"About a month."

"Maybe he took a second shift job *for* an alibi," DeBerry said. He arched his eyebrows, showed his cockeyed grin, then retreated to his office.

Barnes slowly nodded and let out a long, slow breath. "Keep me up to date," he said as he left.

Perhaps Ted *did* take the second job as an alibi. Perhaps he *did* have an accomplice. Both were possibilities. Damn good possibilities. But as Church had heard DeBerry say a hundred times, a theory was just that—a theory. Until it was proven.

Church picked up the phone and dialed the North Carolina Department of Insurance. "Investigator Mauney, please," he said to the receptionist.

"She's out in the field today. I can page her and have her return the call if you'd like."

Church gave the information to the receptionist and hung up. He knew already that the deeper he delved into Patricia's death, the deeper the insurance questions would become.

He could think of no one he'd rather have investigating the insurance end of the case than Ann Mauney. As North Carolina's first female investigator, and for many years the only female to hold the position, Mauney was top of the line. She wasn't only a credit to her gender, she was a credit to the entire North Carolina Department of Insurance.

Church spread a napkin on his desk and reached for the Burger King bag. As he did, his phone rang.

"A Mr. Gary Lyles is here to see you," the department secretary said.

"Oh, good. Send him on back." Church hung up and again set aside his lunch.

He had been anxious to talk to Gary Lyles, the former owner of the building supply store that still bore his name.

Church had met Lyles earlier in the week when he and DeBerry stopped by the store to talk to Ted. Lyles had come up from his retirement home in Long Beach, North Carolina, to help out in the store while Ted made funeral arrangements. But the store had been busy, and their conversation with Lyles had been limited. Now, Church wondered what piece of the puzzle Lyles might offer.

"Detective Church?" Lyles said as he marched into the office and offered his hand. "I hope this isn't a bad time."

"No, not at all. Have a seat."

Lyles was a matter-of-fact man with a strong presence and equally strong body. Church figured him to be in his early sixties, with the physique and hands of a man unafraid of hard work. His gray hair was thinning on top but was thick above his ears. An equally thick, gray mustache dominated his lower face.

"Ah . . . you're a Mason, I see," Lyles said, pointing to the ring Church wore.

Church looked at the similar ring Lyles wore. Their eyes met. Church felt immediately at ease. Lyles was a straightforward man who knew right from wrong, regardless of his relationship with any of the parties.

"I just want you to know, Detective Church, if

there is anything I can do at all to help, I will. I loved that girl like she was my own daughter."

"How long did you know Patricia, Mr. Lyles?"

"Please, call me Gary." Lyles settled back into the chair and turned his gaze upward. "Hmm . . . a few years, I guess. I met her when she and Ted were dating. Actually, I met her before they started dating, when they were *just* friends, as young people like to say."

"How long have you known Ted?"

"Ted I've known since he was a boy. Little guy, maybe ten, eleven. My wife and I were members of his father's church. Helped build the church, actually."

"That would be Monnett Road Baptist?"

Lyles nodded firmly. "Yes, my wife and I were members at Monnett Road until we moved to the beach after I sold the business. We only get up to Greensboro occasionally now."

"You're here this week because of the circumstances?"

"Yes, Ronnie Jr. called me about five o'clock the morning it happened and asked me if I'd come up and take care of the business this week. My wife packed me a bag while I showered. In thirty minutes, I was on the road."

"Ted actually owns the business now, though, correct?"

"That's right. I sold it to him . . . hmm, let's see, I guess it was around the end of '93. It was right before he and Patricia got married. See, Ted had been working for me since he was sixteen. No, excuse me, he was fifteen because his mother used to have to bring him. He didn't have his driver's license yet."

"What kind of worker was Ted?"

Lyles shook his head. "Good worker. Fantastic. Ted's a smart boy. See, I wanted him to have this business, Detective Church. I had kind of taken Ted under my wing when he was growing up, and he looked upon me, I suppose, as sort of a father figure."

"Were things not good with his own father?"

Lyles scratched at his chin and twisted his lips into a frown. "Things were *okay*, I suppose. There was some financial strain. See, Ted's parents married very young. They were just kids themselves, and before they knew it, here they were with two little boys. Raising kids is never easy, you know. Understand, Detective Church, I think the world of these people. They're good, fine people. I just don't always agree with the way they raised their kids.

"Ted would come to me for advice, if he needed to borrow money. You know how teenagers are, always wanting something." Lyles laughed a hearty, genuine laugh.

"You felt comfortable selling Ted the business?"

"Well, yes and no. Ted's a good, hard worker, but he doesn't know how to manage his money very well. I felt comfortable selling him the business after he became engaged to *Patricia*. Now, *that* was a smart girl. I told him, 'You let her handle the books and the money, and y'all are going to be all right'."

"You said after he became engaged to Patricia. Had he been engaged before?"

Lyles laughed. "Oh, you know how teenage boys are. One day they're going to marry this one, the next day it's someone new. But see, I told Ted I'd sell him the business after he got married. I thought marriage would settle him down some, make him a little more responsible. When he started dating Patricia . . . well, of all the young women Ted dated, Patricia was by far the most level-headed. I knew it was a good match, business-wise."

"Did you push him to marry Patricia?"

"No, no . . . I didn't *push* him. But I did encourage it, I suppose. Patricia loved that boy." Lyles shook his head, slowly, thoughtfully. "You could see it in her eyes. The eyes are the windows to the soul, you know, and when they were together, oh boy . . . she couldn't take her eyes off him."

Church leaned back in his chair. "You said you actually met Patricia before they started dating?"

"Yes. See, Ted and Patricia were actually roommates before they started *dating*."

"They lived together before they were married?" This struck Church as odd. It was the first comment he had heard that didn't fit the picture of Patricia's deep religious conviction.

"Just as *roommates*, mind you. They were still just friends at this point. As a matter of fact, Ted was dating other girls, mainly Janet Blakley."

"*Blakley*?"

"Yes, she was Patricia's first cousin. They lived next door to each other when they were children."

"Did Patricia date other men while Ted was living with her?"

A sad smile crept from beneath the thick mustache. Lyles slowly shook his head. "No. Ted was the only man Patricia ever dated. She loved him from the moment she first laid eyes on him."

CHAPTER TWELVE

Last night Ted and I had a great talk—tonight I miss him. He got on to me about exercising, wanted to make sure I was doing it, I guess. What for, I wonder????

Patricia Kimble's journal
January 23, 1992

Summer 1992

"Bringing him lunch again, I see." Gary Lyles shook his head and smiled. What was he going to do with this love-struck young lady?

Patricia smiled shyly, her large brown eyes cast downward. "I cooked dinner last night, and we had some left. I didn't want to throw it away."

"And it just so happens you probably cooked his favorite meal, too?"

Patricia laughed, a soft, sincere laugh that warmed Gary's heart.

"He's out on the floor helping a customer, I think."

Gary laid a handful of cash receipts on his cluttered desk. "He'll be through in a minute."

The office of the building supply store was what one might expect. It was small with paneled walls, dusty, and filled with a cedar scent. Gary Lyles was far more concerned with the business transactions taking place on the sales floor and in the yard than with what went on inside his office, or for that matter, with how the office looked.

"Actually," Patricia said, "it's you I'd like to talk with."

"Me?" Gary feigned surprise, although he knew Patricia knew better. Gary was her confidant, her advisor. He loved her dearly. It wasn't his blood that had given her life, but the bond between a father and daughter couldn't have been stronger. "Have a seat, sweetheart. What's on your mind?"

"I saw an ad in the paper. An ad for a modeling school."

"Modeling school?" After the words were out, he hoped his tone didn't sound discouraging. Not that he disapproved. It was just unusual for Patricia to even consider something so frivolous.

Patricia chuckled as if she had read his mind. "No, I don't want to be a model. But it said that they can teach you how to wear makeup, how to walk, how to make yourself more . . . presentable."

Gary leaned back in his chair and studied her for a moment. And he understood.

Patricia was one of the most beautiful young women he had ever known—on the inside. She had an open, loving heart like no other, a sense of practicality both women and men twice her age would long for, and a strong devotion to God. But Gary was older, more mature. Most men Patricia's age had yet to learn to appreciate a woman's inner beauty.

Gary tried to imagine what a man Patricia's age, a man like Ted, saw when he looked at her. Patricia was heavyset, plain, and wore little, if any, makeup. Her clothes were conservative, almost unfashionable. She wore her brown hair long and straight, void of hours spent with blow-dryers and curlers.

It wasn't that Patricia didn't care about her exterior appearance. Her interest in modeling school proved that. She had other things to worry about, to spend her hard-earned money on. And now, it appeared to Gary that Patricia also had a plan. If the only way to win Ted Kimble's heart was to change the way she looked, that's what this young lady was going to do.

"So, what do you think?" she asked with a shy, uncertain smile. "Ted told me if I lost some weight, he'd take me to the mountains."

Gary wanted to wrap his arms around her and tell her she was beautiful just the way she was. But he didn't. Patricia Blakley loved Ted Kimble so much, the opinions of other men wouldn't matter. "Well, I don't see that it would hurt," Gary said. "There's never any harm in someone wanting to better themselves."

"But it's so expensive. Three hundred dollars!" She laughed as if the amount were absolutely preposterous. "I don't know that I can afford to spend that kind of money on something like . . . well, like this."

Gary tweaked his mustache and gave the matter some thought. "Tell you what—I'll pay for it if you'll go."

"Oh, no! Gary, I never meant for you to pay—"

Gary held up his hand to interrupt her. "I know, I know. But if I pay, then you'll feel obligated to go, right?"

Patricia sighed, then slowly nodded, her pale lips spreading into that same shy smile.

"Who knows?" Gary said, "after taking this course, you'll probably have all sorts of men beating down your door."

Patricia laughed. "There's only one man, though, that I'll let in."

Gary knew that for a fact. He couldn't count the hours of conversations he and Patricia had regarding Ted. She would ask Gary about girls Ted was dating and how they were getting along. Although he knew he should have, Gary never told her to stop waiting in the wings and playing second to any of Ted's latest conquests. No, because Gary wanted Ted to notice Patricia nearly as bad as she did. He loved Ted as if he were his own son and could think of no other woman as good for him as Patricia Blakley. Yes, Gary had told Ted he would sell him the business once he was married. But Gary desperately hoped it would be Patricia, not one of the many pretty little playthings Ted was prone to date.

Late October 1993

The overly energized aerobic instructor's voice competed with the booming, fast-tempo dance music as she shouted commands like a drill sergeant. Patricia's calves throbbed. She looked at the clock. Only ten more minutes. Ten more minutes of torture, she thought and laughed out loud.

"What are you laughing at?" Karen, another of the instructor's victims, asked breathlessly. "Our stupidity?"

Patricia burst out laughing and had to stop to catch her breath.

"Come on, ladies!" the instructor shouted. "Work it!"

Patricia grumbled and fell back into rhythm.

Later, in the locker room, she scrubbed her face at the sink, then looked at herself in the mirror. She smiled. For the first time in her life, she had those little elegant dips between her neck and shoulders.

"Looking good, girl," Karen said.

Patricia smiled softly. "Thanks."

Ted had seemed to notice, too. He had taken her to the mountains, to the beach, even to Disney World. They always had such a good time together. He always made sure she had fun. He could make her laugh about anything. He made her feel special.

Who cared what others thought. She didn't think he was just using her. She truly enjoyed doing things for him. Washing his clothes. Cooking for him. Little things like that would one day make her a good wife, right?

Patricia took the clip from her hair and shook out her newly permed curls. She liked the way the ringlets framed her face. She dropped the towel she had wrapped around herself, then slid into her tight jeans and her lacy bra. She still wasn't quite used to wearing something so, so . . . sexy. But she liked how it made her feel. The bra was an expensive one, too, bought at that little specialty store where Janet bought hers.

CHAPTER THIRTEEN

Janet Blakley stared at the diamond engagement ring. Catching the light from the streetlamp, it seemed to glow from the velvet-lined box. Janet didn't know what to say. Ted had proposed before, on several occasions. But this was the first time he had gone as far as buying a ring.

"Well?" Ted asked. "What do you say?"

Janet looked away from the ring, away from Ted. She wasn't sure what to tell him. Or *how* to tell him. "It's beautiful," she said softly, then mustered her courage. "But I've . . . I've told you all along I wasn't going to get married until I finished college."

"I know, I know. But things could be so good for us now, baby." He lightly stroked her face, his lips lightly brushing hers.

Janet turned away. "Ted, my parents won't pay for my college if I'm married. You know that."

He turned her face toward his and softly kissed her. "They don't have to know."

"What?" Janet jerked away and stared at him in disbelief.

"We don't have to tell them. No one has to know."

She wasn't sure which startled her more: the seriousness in his voice or the absurdity of what he was saying. "I'm not going to do that, Ted. I'm not going to lie to my parents."

Ted sat back in the seat and drummed his fingers on the steering wheel, rising anger pursing his lips. "Look, we can go to Virginia. They don't require twenty-four hours for a blood test. Then, after you graduate, we'll have a big church wedding. The kind you want."

She kept a watchful eye on his expression, on his mounting anger. Still, the idea was absolutely preposterous! "No! I'm not going to do it."

"I told you we'd have a big fancy wedding—"

"It's not that, Ted. It's just that I don't understand the rush. And I don't understand why—"

"Because things have changed, Janet. That's why." He glared at her, then stared out the window. "Gary's wanting to retire soon. He's wanting to sell the business."

"What's that got to do with us?"

Ted huffed and hesitated a moment before answering. "He won't sell me the business until I'm married."

Her expression dissolved into sadness. A million thoughts ran through her mind, each in the shape of a dollar sign. "So, I'm the key to a business deal?"

Ted turned in the seat and reached for her hand, but she pulled back. "Come on, don't think of it like that, Janet. We were planning on getting married after you graduated, anyway. We'll just up the date a little, that's all." He kissed the tip of her nose, her cheek, her chin, his lips slowly reaching hers.

But there was a distance in her response. A distance caused by something other than his proposal.

"What's the matter?" he asked, lifting her chin with his finger.

"I don't know, Ted." She was hesitating, searching for the right words. "I haven't been real comfortable with the whole situation lately."

"What situation?"

"You, me. Patricia."

"*Patricia?* What about her?"

Janet nearly laughed. Not because it was funny. She nearly laughed because it was so sad. "She loves you, Ted. Everyone knows that. Everyone can see it."

"I can't help that. Besides, Patricia knows her and me are just friends. And she knows how I feel about you."

"But she's my cousin, Ted. I love her. I don't want to see her hurt."

"So I'm not supposed to love you because Patricia has some kind of crush on me?"

"It's more than a crush, Ted. You know that. Look at her. Look at what she's done with herself."

Ted had to admit the changes were remarkable. Patricia had lost so much weight, she was now nearly as small as Janet. And her hair. It now fell in long, loose curls. Just like Janet's. Had he openly compared plain, plump Patricia to Janet enough that maybe Patricia had gotten the hint? Oh well. Whatever her reasons, they weren't his concern. Janet was his only concern.

"And with you living there with her, it just encourages—"

"Then I'll move out," he said.

Janet sighed and turned away. "It's not just that. It's not only Patricia." She hesitated again, then finally said what had been toying with her for weeks. "I think it's time we see other people."

The comment nearly knocked the breath from him.

"I'm here at college," Janet continued in a quiet voice. "And you're back home. I just think it would be the best thing for everyone right now."

Ted snapped the ring box closed and shoved it into his pocket.

Janet knew the warning signs and tried to soothe his rising temper. "I'll be home for Thanksgiving in a few weeks. Maybe we can talk about it some more then."

Ted nodded and started the car.

Janet sat near the back in the sanctuary of South Elm Street Baptist Church. It was Thanksgiving weekend. A festive air filled the church, the pews filled to capacity.

Janet had enjoyed her time at home. Her mother Linda had prepared a huge meal for Janet, her father John, and Janet's two younger sisters. Since she had been away at college, Janet had grown to cherish the closeness of family, especially during the holidays.

She had bypassed Sunday school but had arrived in time for the 11:00 service. Now Janet waited patiently for it to begin, sitting alone, lost in her own thoughts. She and Ted had yet to talk. As a matter of fact, she hadn't even seen him since she'd been home. It really didn't matter, she supposed. She hadn't changed her mind. Still, she didn't want to leave things the way they were, in limbo.

Low but excited voices near the hallway doors drew her from her quiet thoughts. Patricia and a small group of women from her Sunday school class gathered for a moment at the doorway, then entered the sanctuary. Patricia was radiant, beaming a smile as bright as Janet had ever seen. A group of young men, including Ted, followed behind the women. Some of them paired off into couples and took their seats along the crowded pews.

Ted sat down beside Patricia in a pew a few rows in front of Janet. They probably didn't even see me, Janet thought. Just as well. There was nothing to be gained by adding stress to the situation.

The reverend took the pulpit and welcomed the congregation. After a hymn of Thanksgiving, he began the announcements. Janet listened halfheartedly, but one announcement caused her to jerk her head up and listen. She couldn't believe what she was hearing!

"It is with great love in my heart," the reverend said, "that I announce the engagement of Miss Patricia Gail Blakley and Mr. Theodore Mead Kimble."

Smiles flowed freely throughout the church as Janet fought hard to regain the breath that had just been knocked out of her. She caught a glimpse of the ring Patricia proudly displayed. It was the same ring Ted had offered *her* only two weeks earlier!

Janet's heart was beating so furiously, she was certain everyone in the sanctuary could hear it. Her breath was coming in shallow gasps. Her eyes batted back a swell of tears.

As soon as the congregation stood for the next hymn, Janet scooted around the worshipers who shared her pew and walked toward the door. Just remain calm, she told herself, as she tried to control her pace.

Once outside, away from view, she burst into tears. They were tears for herself, for her embarrassment, for her hurt. But mostly, they were tears for Patricia.

CHAPTER FOURTEEN

Church straightened the tie of his uniform. This was one off-duty assignment he couldn't refuse.

Hanes-Lineberry Funeral Home had called the day before and asked for help with traffic at a scheduled visitation. Judging from the number of calls they had received and the popularity of the deceased, they felt an uniformed officer was warranted.

Flowers in abundance spread their scent. Bouquets of helium-filled purple balloons covered the ceiling. Patricia had loved balloons, purple ones the most. She had kept a helium tank beside her desk at Cinnamon Ridge. Children, new residents, anyone Patricia felt could use a little pick-me-up received a balloon.

Church checked the video camera DeBerry had secured in the back wall of the room where Patricia's urn sat. Each person entering to pay his or her respects would be documented. The sergeant had arranged with the funeral home to copy the register book, hoping to match the names with the faces from the video.

Assured the camera was working and that everything was set, Church stepped outside.

The Kimbles were the first to arrive. As Ted approached, he glanced at Church once, then again, holding the gaze until it became a stare.

"Ted," Church said and politely nodded. Edna Kimble shuffled her son toward the door.

Moments later, the Blakleys arrived. Reuben and Kristy flanked Sheila, helping to steady her. Another car pulled in directly behind the Blakleys. A middle-aged couple, James and Judy Stump, got out from the front seat. Their daughter and her husband, Kimberly and Ronnie Kimble, got out of the back. Ronnie was wearing his dress blues, his face tightly drawn as tears streamed down his face.

Church studied Ronnie, unsure of the young Marine's name or his relationship to Patricia. They had yet to meet, but the detective recognized him from the night at the church. He was the young man who sobbed openly, clinging to Bertha Blakley.

"Detective Church," Reuben said as he, Kristy, and Sheila approached the steps. "What are you doing here?"

"Helping direct traffic." Church shook Reuben's hand and offered his condolences, then asked, "Who is the guy in the Marine uniform?"

Reuben glanced over his shoulder. "Ted's brother, Ronnie."

Once the rush of traffic was over, Church stepped into the hallway and scanned the receiving room.

Still, Ted was showing little emotion. In fact, Church thought, he was almost jovial. He laughed and chatted casually. He smiled and shook the hands of mourners as if it were a high school reunion.

Ted wasn't the only one who didn't seem to grasp the loss. Edna stood proudly by her son's side, smiling as if she were in the receiving line of a wedding.

"Yep, she's in there," Ted told the crowd as he lifted the urn that contained Patricia's ashes.

"I bet she weighs a lot less now than she did," Edna said, and the two chuckled.

Church swallowed the bile that surged from his stomach. He looked at Sheila Blakley, the tiny woman who seemed so lost. He couldn't shake the image of her collapsing to the ground. He couldn't erase the memory of her pain-filled eyes, a pain deeper than he could ever imagine. Those eyes, bearing the total depth of a mother's sorrow, had burned themselves deep into his mind, and his soul.

The line of visitors wound its way through the room, into the hallway and out the main door. Church studied each face, watched their movements, observed whom they spoke to. But one he kept going back to. One in particular. Ronnie Kimble.

Where his brother Ted had shown little emotion, Ronnie was overcome with grief. His chiseled shoulders heaved and sagged with each sob, contradicting his dress blue uniform, the image of a rock solid Marine. He stood in the receiving line next to his family, but it was the Blakleys from whom he sought comfort. They seemed as perplexed about his outpouring of emotion as they were at their reason for being there.

Strange. The brother-in-law shows more grief than the husband does, Church thought.

But it was just another example of how far apart

the Kimble brothers were. The only thing they had in common was a last name and a bloodline. If Ted were day, Ronnie was night.

For years, Ronnie had walked in the looming shadow of his brother and struggled to find his own way. The U.S. Marine Corps was his first step. In April 1993, Ronnie joined the Marines shortly after a breakup with a girlfriend, Michelle Parker, to prove to others and to himself that he was his own man.

But it wasn't just his brother's shadow Ronnie struggled with. He struggled in school. He struggled to fit in with others. He struggled to gain his parents', especially his mother's, acceptance.

In school, Ronnie was labeled a slow learner and was held back in kindergarten. In the fourth grade, he was diagnosed as learning disabled. According to the counselor, Ronnie was incredibly high strung, compulsive, and very talkative, all of which impaired his ability to learn. Although it was never medically proven, Ron and Edna blamed their youngest son's problems on high fevers and seizures he had suffered as an infant.

Although Ronnie was physically strong, he wasn't terribly athletic. He chose to spend his afternoons and weekends mowing yards or doing odd jobs to earn his spending money. The elderly adored the clean-cut boy with the smile too big for his narrow face and didn't mind parting with a dollar to have him clean up around their yards.

He related well to children much younger than himself, too. In fact, Ronnie occasionally taught the Sunday school class for six- to eight-year-olds at his father's church.

It was there, Monnett Road Baptist Church, where he found favor in a young girl named Kimberly Stump. Kimberly's parents, James and Judy Stump, were members of Monnett. Their young daughter was taken with Ronnie's bright eyes and broad smile. They dated off and on through high school, but their relationship was based more on a deep friendship than romance. After Ronnie joined the Marines following his breakup with Michelle Parker, he traveled nearly every weekend from Camp Lejeune to attend his parent's church. He and Kimberly renewed their friendship, but this time it went much further than casual dating.

James and Judy Stump had their reservations. They liked Ronnie—everyone liked Ronnie—but they were concerned about their daughter's future. They, like every other member of Monnett Road Baptist Church, saw the blatant favoritism paid to Ted by the boys' parents and worried about the long-term emotional effects on Ronnie. But Ronnie was a good kid. Everyone saw that, too. Older members of the church took him under their wings and openly showed the love-starved boy the affection he craved, and needed.

In September of 1994, Ronnie and Kimberly were married. Ronnie returned to Camp Lejeune. Kimberly stayed behind.

Now, at the funeral home, Kimberly stayed close to her parents while her husband continually poured his sympathies on the anguished Blakley family.

The visitation was scheduled to end at 9:00, but the long line of people wishing to pay their respects still extended well into the parking lot. Not until after 11:00 did the crowd begin to thin.

Although the funeral home had officially released Church from his assignment, he hung around until the Kimbles and Blakleys were ready to leave. Around midnight, the families gathered the balloons and carried them outside into a cold, drizzling rain. Simultaneously, they released the purple, helium-filled balloons, watching through the rain and their tears as the balloons rose into the darkness.

"She would have liked that," Richard said, his lips trembling with emotion.

Church waited a few minutes, then called Reuben aside. "Tell me about Ronnie Kimble," he asked quietly.

Reuben shrugged. "I don't really know him that well. Just through Ted. He's all right, I guess."

"Is he always this emotional?"

Reuben looked back at Ronnie. The young Marine was embracing Bertha Blakley, crying childlike on the frail woman's shoulder. "Believe it or not, he was worse the night at the church."

Church studied the scene for a moment. Something just didn't make sense. "How'd he get to the church so fast? Camp Lejeune's a four-hour drive."

"He didn't come from Camp Lejeune. He was home on leave."

CHAPTER FIFTEEN

The following morning, Church stared out his living-room window at the soft rain pattering against the glass. In a few hours, a memorial service for Patricia would begin at South Elm Street Baptist Church. Afterward, life would go on. There would come a day, some day, that the Blakleys would smile again, maybe even laugh. Christmases would be celebrated, summer cookouts attended. But it would never be the same.

"What are you doing?" Brenda asked her husband. Her sudden presence startled him.

"Oh, just thinking."

She pushed aside the curtain partially covering the window and peered outside. "What are you looking at?"

"Nothing, really." It didn't matter what he looked at anymore. All he saw was Sheila Blakley's pitiful eyes.

Brenda let the curtain fall back into place and glanced quizzically at her husband. "The washer's making that noise again. Will you look at *it* when you get through? I've got a ton of laundry to do today."

Church nodded. Life goes on, he thought, and turned away from the window.

"Breakfast is ready," Brenda said, heading toward the kitchen. "Come on and eat before it gets cold."

Church sat down at the table and picked at his breakfast. With washing machines to fix, laundry that needing washing, dishes to do—he wondered what exactly made a family *normal.* He kept going back to a comment Gary Lyles had made about Ted and Ronnie's parents, Ron and Edna Kimble: *When you're just kids yourselves.* Church wondered if the Kimble's young age influenced the way their children were raised, or whether the outcome was some sort of destiny.

Ron and Edna Kimble had married young. Too young, some would say. Ron was only seventeen, his young bride but fifteen, when they exchanged vows. A year later, still babies themselves, they were parents. Then, only two years after Ted was born, younger brother Ronnie Jr. followed.

For eight years, the young couple labored in a mill in Mebane, North Carolina, about twenty miles northwest of Greensboro. Riddled with family responsibilities, Ron took to the bottle for solace, often leaving Edna to tend to the two boys alone.

One day, the strain became too much. The burdensome responsibilities and the alcohol fueled an explosive argument. Young Ted witnessed his father slap his mother. Whether out of protection, pity, or love, a strange and undeniable bond soon formed between

Ted and his mother, often leaving little Ronnie to fend for himself.

At twenty-six, disgusted with his life and with himself, Ron Sr. put down the bottle and turned to a higher source. He gave his life to Jesus Christ and answered a call into the ministry. He and Edna packed up the two boys, left the mill behind, and moved to Lynchburg, Virginia, where Ron enrolled at Liberty University's Bible School. The boys, now eight and six, were enrolled in a private Christian school. Under the watchful eye of the university's chancellor, Dr. Jerry Falwell, and now with a new purpose and new hope, Ron seemed to turn his life around. The family often took weekend trips to Washington, D.C.

Still, like the old Baptist saying, "God never promised you a rose garden," life wasn't easy for the Kimbles.

After graduation, Ron Sr. moved his family to a trailer park on the outskirts of Pleasant Garden and sought a church in need of a minister. Though the area was rich in Baptist believers, finding a church was difficult. The young minister made several attempts at starting his own church, often holding services in a vacated storefront. Although the Lord provided their basic needs, the family continued to struggle financially.

Finally, Ron Sr.'s prayer was answered. In Monnett Road Baptist Church the Kimbles found their place. It was a small church, an older, one-room, white-framed building. Located in Julian, North Carolina, just a few miles south of Pleasant Garden, the church's congregation was just as small, but they were good-hearted, simple country folks.

The parishioners instantly took to their new pastor's young family, particularly his two sons. Ted and Ronnie Kimble were the most well-mannered, most polite little boys they had ever met.

CHAPTER SIXTEEN

The Monday after Patricia's memorial service, Church turned off Highway 22 onto Branchwater Road. Fenced pasture lined both sides of the dirt road. Holstein cattle grazed under the shade of fall foliage on one side, quarter horses clustered together on the other. A few farmhouses, most as old as the road they lined, were separated by the rolling farmland.

Richard Blakley and his mother Bertha lived alone in the last house on the left. The house Patricia had grown up in. The house her mother Sheila had left.

Today, it wasn't Richard that Church wanted to see. He pulled into the driveway of the house next door to see Richard's niece, Janet Blakley.

Church knocked on the front door of the two-story, white-frame house and waited only a second before the door opened.

"Janet?" Church asked, as he had yet to meet the young lady in person.

"Yes," she said, her voice barely above a whisper. Janet had been fearful when Church spoke with her on the phone. Now her large brown eyes reflected the same fear.

Janet peered at him from behind the door she held only partially open. Her complexion was as fair as porcelain. Her face was a palette of delicate, feminine features.

"I'm Detective Jim Church with the Guilford County Sheriff's Department."

Janet glanced over her shoulder into the house, still holding the door only halfway open.

"Tell you what," Church said, "why don't we go for a walk?" He didn't know the root of her nervousness but it was obvious she was hesitant to talk to him in the house.

She nodded quickly. The auburn curls that spiraled midway down her back bounced with the movement. "Okay. Give me just a second to grab a jacket." She closed the door, then reappeared a moment later. She wore snug jeans that outlined her slender frame and a lightweight jacket over a silky blouse. Her makeup was flawless: her lips were perfectly lined with color, a whisper of rose-colored blush highlighted her prominent cheekbones. Church wondered if she looked this perfect every morning.

They stepped off the porch and followed the dirt driveway around to the back of the house. They continued along the path, well past the house, before Janet spoke. "Sorry about this," she said. "I assume you want to talk about Ted, and there are things I'd rather my parents not hear."

"No problem." Church dropped his hands into his pockets and took in the landscape. He took a slow breath, enjoying the cleanliness of the country air.

"You've got some beautiful land out here."

"It's nice. And quiet. I like walking out here sometimes when I just need to get away."

They walked a little further. Then Church said, "Tell me about your relationship with Ted."

Janet took a deep breath, then slowly began. She told him how they met in school, how they started dating, and how Patricia fit into the picture. Where Patricia was concerned, Janet echoed what Gary Lyles had said.

"Did their engagement and marriage cause hard feelings between you and Patricia?" Church asked.

"I wouldn't really call it *hard feelings*, but our relationship was strained for a while. It was just kind of awkward."

"Did you see Ted and Patricia much after they were married?"

Janet shook her head. "Not really. I mean, I'd see them occasionally, at a few family gatherings—the ones they'd come to, anyway. Things like that."

"What do mean by the *ones they'd come to*?"

"They did more things with Ted's parents than with our family. They were always going out to dinner with Ted's mother and father, or going here or there with them. That's how it was with a lot of Ted's girlfriends. Ted had a habit of pulling you away from your own family."

"Did he do that with you?"

"He tried. To some extent, he succeeded. But his mother didn't like me too much." She chuckled, but it was a sad, tiny sound. "She adored Patricia, though."

"Why didn't she like you?"

Janet turned her face to the sun, then looked at Church. "I was too independent."

Church smiled. He didn't doubt that for a minute. Janet Blakley was smart, confident, and could probably choose any man she wanted.

"She didn't like me because I didn't pick up after Ted, or go out of my way to cook for him, or do all those little things she felt a woman should do for her man. I just didn't take any crap from him, and she didn't like that. I guess I should have been more subservient." She smiled a warm smile.

"Do you regret that you weren't?"

"Lord, no. If I had been, it probably would have been my body they found."

Church stopped and stared at her for a moment. Was Janet simply saying she would have rather died before allowing a man to control her life? Or was she implying there was some sort of master plan in which Ted was involved? "I'm not sure I understand what you mean."

She pushed a stray lock of curls from her eyes and gazed at him. "I think he had it planned from the start."

"Ted?"

She slowly nodded. "He wanted that business more than anything."

Looking squarely at Janet, Church shielded his eyes from the bright sunlight, then asked, "Are you saying you think Ted was responsible for Patricia's death?"

Janet looked away and smiled, then gazed back at Church. "Don't you?"

They had stopped along the path at a three-sided barn. Yard rakes, shovels, and long-handled hoes hung on pegs nailed into the side wall. Shelves built into the back wall held rows of mason jars filled with garden-grown vegetables. The aroma of the dirt floor pleased Church's senses, momentarily taking him back to the Blue Ridge Mountains.

"Your mama do a lot of canning?" he asked, leaning against the rear tire of a John Deere tractor.

"Always," Janet laughed. She sat down on a wooden yard swing at the edge of the barn.

"Mine did, too. Heck, when I was a kid, I don't ever remember eating anything that didn't come out of the garden."

Janet softly smiled and pulled her jacket together, warding off the early-morning chill. "You don't think Ted's responsible for Patricia's death?" she quietly asked.

Church grinned. "We're still in the very early stages of our investigation. Right now, everyone's a suspect." He lightly kicked at the dirt floor, savoring the smell that wafted upward. "What makes *you* think Ted had something to do with it?"

"Because I know him. Ted will stop at nothing to get what he wants."

"But he got what he wanted, didn't he? He got the business, right?"

"Yeah, but that was only good for a little while. Ted's the kind that wants more, more, and then more. He's never satisfied with what he's got."

Church absorbed the information, then asked, "Have you ever known him to be violent?"

Janet shook her head. "No, not really. Not with me, anyway. I mean, he's got a temper, but he never physically hurt me. Although he was very . . ."

Church waited for her to continue, but when she didn't, he pressed her. "He was very what?"

"He was . . ." she hesitated and gathered her words. "He was very pushy. Sexually."

"Did he ever force himself on you?"

Janet stared off into the field and slowly shook her head. "No, he never forced me. But I could see how it might happen with someone else. Someone maybe not so strong-willed." She gently pushed her toe into the ground, softly rocking the swing back and forth. "Ted has this way of getting whatever he wants. It doesn't matter who he hurts, or even whether its legal."

"You mean murder?"

"That and other things. I know a few years ago he did stuff like scratching his own car and then filing an insurance claim on it. Or one time he actually broke into his own car and reported his stereo stolen. Stuff like that."

"No one ever questioned it?"

"His mother works in the loss department of an insurance company. I'm sure he knew how to get around the questions."

So the insurance claim he filed when the house was broken into wasn't the first false claim he had filed, Church thought. Was it possible Ted had advanced from collecting on simple insurance claims by keying his own car, to reporting expensive jewelry as stolen, to the granddaddy of all—murdering his spouse to collect life insurance? It was like climbing a ladder: you have to start at the bottom rung before you can reach the top.

But Ted Kimble had a solid alibi. No matter how

hard he tried to figure around it, Church couldn't deny it.

Church strolled out of the barn and gazed over the landscape. "Tell me about Ted's brother, Ronnie."

"He's nice enough, I suppose. Kind of odd, though."

"What do you mean by *odd*?"

She shrugged her shoulders. "I mean, he's friendly and all, he's probably *too* friendly. He's just kind of . . . strange. Some people would say his elevator don't go all the way to the top." She softly grinned and batted her eyes as if she were ashamed of her less than favorable characterization.

"Are you saying he's mentally impaired?"

"Well, I don't mean he's retarded or anything like that. He's just . . . slow. He was always in the special classes in school. I mean, good gosh, he was almost eighteen years old when he was still in the tenth grade."

"How was his relationship with Ted?"

"Typical brothers. They hate each other as much as they love each other."

"Did they get along?"

She shook her head. "Not really. Ted was the older brother, the *cool* one. Ronnie was always the geeky, little brother, and Ted took advantage of it."

"What do you mean?"

"He pushed him around a lot. He wasn't always nice to him. A lot of people felt sorry for Ronnie because of it."

"Their parents didn't do anything to stop it?"

Janet laughed. "Ted was the favorite son. Anyone that knows them will tell you that. If they did something good, Ted got the praise. If they did something bad, Ronnie got the blame. It really is kind of sad in a way."

"Have you ever known Ronnie to get violent?"

Again, she shook her head. "Not really. I've never seen it, but . . ."

"But what?" Church asked.

"Well, I don't know the whole story, but there was this girl he dated in high school. Actually, I think Ted dated her, too. I know Ted dated her twin sister, anyway. But I heard that Ronnie may have gotten violent with her."

"Do you know the story behind it?"

"No, not really. I heard she got pregnant, and he didn't want the baby. You really need to talk to her about it, though. She can tell you a lot more than I can. Her name's Michelle Parker."

CHAPTER SEVENTEEN

Church tracked down Michelle Parker at an apartment complex in northeast Greensboro. She kept the chain lock on the door and peered through the slim opening. A baby cried in the background.

"Michelle?" Church asked.

She was hesitant to answer and eyed Church cautiously.

"I'm Detective Jim Church with the Guilford County Sheriff's Department. I'm looking for Michelle Parker."

The baby's cries grew louder, and Michelle glanced over her shoulder. "Yeah, what do you want with me?" she asked, turning back to Church. She pursed thick lips in a display of attitude.

"I want to talk to you about Ted and Ronnie Kimble. I understand you're an acquaintance of theirs."

Her expression tightened. Her eyes grew wide.

"I'm investigating the death of Ted's wife and was hoping you could give me some insight."

"Look, I knew Ted and Ronnie a long time ago. I

doubt I could tell you anything." She started to close the door, but Church stuck his foot in the way.

"Michelle—I need your help."

She stared at the foot blocking the door, then glanced again over her shoulder.

"Please, Michelle. It's very important that I talk with you."

"I told you I knew them a long time ago." Her voice quivered, betraying her nail-tough attitude. "I've moved on with my life now. I'm married and have a new baby, and I don't want to drag up the past."

"Your husband doesn't know about Ronnie or Ted, does he?"

She shot Church a look filled with fear. "No," she said quietly, almost a whisper.

"Is he at home?"

She shook her head slowly. "No, not right now, but he may come home for lunch."

"It'll only take a few minutes. Promise."

"I gotta feed the baby."

"You can feed him while we talk. Okay?"

She ran a bone-thin hand over her dark red hair and slowly massaged her forehead. "I don't know . . ."

"We're wasting valuable time." Church spoke in an understanding voice. "And I don't think that baby's going to wait much longer." He smiled a soft smile.

She slowly unlatched the chain and opened the door. "You've got to be out of here by noon, okay?"

"Deal." Church stepped into the apartment and closed the door behind him. The baby, clad only in a sagging diaper and stained T-shirt, squirmed in a tattered playpen in the middle of the cluttered living room. He kicked his chubby legs, scrunched his cherry-red face, and wailed.

"Have a seat. I've got to get his bottle." She disappeared into the kitchen and returned moments later.

Church sat down in a well-worn chair.

Michelle, with the baby, sat across from him on a thread-bare sofa. "So," she said, popping the bottle into the baby's mouth. "What do you want to know?"

"Tell me about your relationship with Ted and Ronnie."

"He's a son of a bitch. What else do you want to know?"

Church read through her toughness and saw a nervous little girl. "Who? Ted or Ronnie?"

She smirked. It was filled with more sadness than attitude. "Both, I guess. Ted probably more than Ronnie, though. Ted's mean. Ronnie's just psycho."

"It's my understanding that you dated both of them?"

She sighed heavily and nodded.

"At different times?"

"Some." She wiped spittle from the baby's mouth with her finger. "I dated Ted first, then I started dating Ronnie. But Ted kept coming around, you know. I ain't proud of it, but he wouldn't leave me alone."

"Did Ronnie know you were still seeing Ted?"

Slowly, she shook her head. "If he did, he never did say."

"What did you mean when you said Ted was mean?"

"He just is. He uses people. And he don't care who he hurts." She shifted her weight and tucked a leg up under her bottom.

"You mean physically or emotionally?"

"Both, I guess. I mean, he never hurt us like beating on us or anything, but he used us."

"Who is *us?*"

"Me and my sister. He dated us both." Tears pooled in her large eyes. "He thought it was so *cool* to do twins."

"You both slept with him?" Church asked in a calming, matter-of-fact tone.

She quickly glanced up at him. "I ain't proud of it, you know. But he was the first. For both of us. We weren't but fifteen. Then we found out he went around bragging about it and it hurt, you know."

Church nodded. He wasn't there to pass judgment on the poor girl. He hoped Michelle knew that. "Where is your sister now?"

Tears ran down Michelle's cheek, and she quickly wiped them away. "She's dead. She got killed in a car wreck."

The baby had finished his bottle and now lay sleeping in his mother's arms. Michelle set the bottle aside and slid her index finger into the grip of her tiny son's hand.

"You want to tell me about another pregnancy you had, Michelle?"

She slowly gazed up at Church, then looked away. The question took her back to a time she would rather forget.

Fall 1989 8:30 A.M.

Michelle paced across her living-room floor, her long, slender legs moving quickly. Was she doing the right thing? Aborting a baby hadn't been an easy decision to come to, and she still had her doubts. Plenty of them.

She knew she wasn't the first teenager to get herself into this situation. She knew girls who had abortions; she also knew girls who had the baby. Neither was an easy road. Michelle knew that. But wasn't it kind of selfish to end an innocent life because you might miss the prom or a Friday night football game? But it's best for the baby, a lot of folks would say. What kind of life would it have, anyway? At least it would have a life, Michelle thought.

She glanced at her watch. Where was he? He should have been here by now.

Ronnie knew the appointment was at 9:00. They had scheduled it that way so she would have plenty of time to get back home and settled before her parents got off work. The lady at the clinic had told her she would probably need to take it easy and stay in bed the rest of the afternoon. Michelle had planned to tell her mother that she wasn't feeling well, that maybe she was coming down with something.

She hated lying to her parents. Hated the deception.

Maybe Ronnie had changed his mind? After all, he was just as confused and scared as she was. He was no more ready to be a father than she was a mother, but deep in their hearts, neither of them was comfortable with even the word *abortion*.

Perhaps she'd talk with Ronnie when he arrived. Was he having just as many doubts?

She softly stroked her belly and wondered if the baby she carried was a boy or a girl. Would it have her dark, olive-toned complexion? Would it be tall and lanky like Ronnie and herself, or stocky . . . like Ted?

She pushed *that* thought out of her mind. It was best if Ronnie didn't even know that possibility existed.

She glanced at her watch. Eight-forty-five. "Damn, where is he?" She had no more spoken the words when a car pulled into her driveway. She recognized the car immediately. It wasn't Ronnie's. It was Ted's.

"Oh, my God! What's he doing here?" Michelle went cold all over. "He wasn't even supposed to know." A surge of panic raced through her body as Ronnie got out of the passenger side and hurried up the walkway. Ted sat behind the wheel, the engine still running.

She met Ronnie at the door. "What's he doing here?" she demanded.

"He's just gonna drive us. I thought I could sit with you in the backseat when it's over." Ronnie was extremely nervous. His words came fast as he glanced back several times at the waiting car. "You ready?"

"Ronnie—I wanted to talk to you. I'm not so sure about this. I don't know if it's what we want."

Ronnie looked back over his shoulder again. Ted was tapping his fingers on the steering wheel. He raced the engine.

"Ronnie, please. Let's just talk about it for a minute, okay?"

He shuffled from one foot to the other and ran his hand over his hair, again and again. "Okay, all right. We'll talk about it in the car."

"With Ted? Why can't we just talk about it here?"

"Michelle, come on. It's not like he doesn't know. We'll talk about it on the way."

To Michelle's sorrow, it was clear Ronnie hadn't changed his mind. But how could he, with big brother Ted around?

She grabbed her purse and followed Ronnie to the car. He opened the front passenger door for her. She looked at him for a moment with surprise. "I'll just sit in the back with you."

"Just get in," Ted snapped. "I'll look like a damn chauffeur if both of you ride in the backseat."

Hesitantly, Michelle slid into the front seat. Ronnie closed the door and slid in behind her. Ted threw the gears in reverse and squealed out of the driveway. Tears rolled down Michelle's face, and she hurriedly wiped them away with the back of her hand.

"What are you crying for?" Ted asked, his voice harsh and cold. "You ain't having second thoughts are you?"

Michelle didn't answer. The tears kept coming.

"Look, I know it's tough," Ted said. His voice had changed as quickly as he had raced out of the driveway. "It's the best thing for both of you, you know?"

Michelle sniffled. She couldn't stop the tears. Who was Ted Kimble to say what was best for her? Or for Ronnie, for that matter. She stared out the passenger-side window. Did Ted suspect the baby could be his?

"Look at my own mom and dad," Ted said. "They got married when they were just kids, you know, and it's always been a struggle for them. For us. You don't want your own kid to have to go through that, do you? Ronnie, you remember." He glanced in the rearview mirror. "There ain't never been enough money."

Ronnie didn't respond. Michelle turned and peered over her shoulder into the backseat. Ronnie's own eyes were now streaked red and glistened with wetness.

They rode the rest of the way in silence. The clinic was only a couple of miles from Michelle's house, so it took only a few minutes to get there. A wave of nausea slammed her hard as Ted pulled into the parking lot. She covered her mouth with her hand, afraid she would vomit. It wasn't the same queasy feeling that had plagued her the last couple of weeks. This was an all-enveloping sickness.

"Well," Ted said, "we're here. Nine o'clock. Right on the nose." He pulled into one of the many available spaces and cut off the car.

Michelle turned and looked at Ronnie. He looked away and stared out the window. "Ronnie . . . we need to talk."

"Talk about what?" Ted snapped. "There's nothing to talk about. Now go on, before you're late."

Michelle jerked her head toward Ted. "I want to talk to Ronnie."

"I said there ain't nothing to talk about. Now, go on."

Ronnie got out of the car and slammed the door. He opened Michelle's door and stood there, holding it open, tapping his foot nervously against the pavement. His gaze darted from Ted to Michelle to the ground.

"Go on. *Now*." There was a firmness in Ted's voice, a harshness that angered Michelle.

"Will you just shut up! This is between me and Ronnie, anyway."

Ted grabbed her arm and dug his fingers into her tender flesh. Michelle tried to jerk away, but Ted tightened his grip. "Don't ever tell me to shut up! You got that, bitch?" He squeezed tighter and gave a painful twist. "Now get your scrawny ass in there before you screw everything up."

"Stop it!" Michelle shouted as she tried to pull away. "You're hurting me!" She squirmed and tried to kick at him, but he blocked her thrusting leg.

"Get in the car, Ronnie, and shut the door!" Ted yanked Michelle closer to him, away from the passenger side. Ronnie frantically glanced around the parking lot. "Get in the damn car, stupid!" Ted yelled.

Ronnie slid into the front seat, pinning Michelle between the two of them.

"I want to talk to Ronnie! Alone!" Michelle screamed.

"Michelle, just shut up!" Ronnie said. He buried his face in his hands, hiding from the chaos.

"Ronnie . . ." Michelle wrestled her arm away from Ted, but he grabbed her by the back of the head, clutching a handful of hair. She screamed in pain, then froze in fear.

She couldn't see it, but she felt the pressure as Ted pressed the barrel of a handgun below her left ear. Ted yanked her head closer, driving the gun deeper.

"Listen, you fucking little bitch—you're gonna have this abortion. You got that?" He pushed harder.

Fear paralyzed her, prohibiting any movement.

"Our daddy's a fucking preacher, and you ain't gonna embarrass my family." He twisted her hair, driving the gun even deeper. "You got that, bitch? You got it, right? Let me hear you say you got it."

She tried to nod but his hold hindered any movement. "Yes," she whimpered.

"Good. 'Cause I'd really hate to have to kill you. Now, do I need to walk your little ass in there?"

A rush of tears poured onto her cheeks. "No." Her voice was nothing more than a faint whisper.

"Then let's get the show on the road." He released his grip and smoothed down her hair. Her skin crawled as he lowered the gun, slowly tracing her neckline, her shoulder, finally resting at her breast.

She shut her eyes for a moment and said a prayer of forgiveness for the life she was about to take. And a prayer of gratitude for the life that had just been spared.

CHAPTER EIGHTEEN

"Dr. Holmes?" Church asked.

The response on the other end of the line was quick. "This is he."

Church introduced himself, then said, "I attended a seminar you held in Greensboro, North Carolina, a few years ago and was wondering if I could get your opinion on a suspect in a homicide I'm currently working?"

"Sure," Holmes answered without hesitation. "What have you got?"

Dr. Ronald Holmes was the founder of the National Institute for the Study of Unsolved Homicides. He worked out of the University of Kentucky at Louisville and was an expert in the field of profiling. The man's knowledge and ability had made a lasting impression on Church.

Church slid his chair closer to his desk and began. "The victim was a twenty-eight-year-old white female. She was shot once in the head and her body set on fire."

Holmes took a long breath, then exhaled. "You're looking for someone from a religious background."

"Pardon?" The answer caught Church off-guard. He wasn't expecting it so quickly. Or, although he was trying to maintain an open mind, maybe it was exactly what he was expecting.

"You're looking for someone from a religious background. Someone who probably grew up in the church."

Church took a second to collect the thoughts running rampant through his mind. "Why do you say that?"

"The fire. There's a twofold reason. The first is, naturally, to cover the crime. The second is, to a person with deep religious roots, in their twisted sort of way, the fire can be an act of cleansing."

"You mean like redemption?"

"Redemption, forgiveness—it's all the same. They're cleansing themselves of the sin they know they've just committed."

As soon as he hung up, Church drove out to Julian, North Carolina. Particularly Monnett Road. It was time, he thought, to introduce himself to Mr. and Mrs. Ronnie Lee Kimble Jr.

Julian was a quiet rural community south of Pleasant Garden. Pleasant Garden, Julian, and Climax, another neighboring farm community, were all equal in size and character. The three villages formed a triangle of farms and undeveloped land that dominated the southeast corner of the county. Their residents shared the same schools, churches, and values.

Church turned off Old Liberty Road onto Monnett Road and slowed the car to a crawl as he passed Monnett Road Baptist Church. The original church, a white wood-sided building, was connected by a covered walkway to a new brick sanctuary. Church assumed the little white building, with its small front porch and wrought-iron handrails, was now used either for Sunday school or perhaps as a fellowship hall. A large lighted sign near the road displayed the church's name. Underneath that was the name Pastor Ron L. Kimble Sr.

Ronnie's house was only a mile or so past the church. It was a single-wide mobile home, a newer model, sitting at the end of a loose-graveled drive. Unopened boxes of vinyl underpinning were stacked in what was to be the front yard. A track on which to mount the underpinning ran partially across the front of the trailer, stopping short at a set of concrete steps. A few tree stumps yet to be cleared stuck up from the ground surrounding the home.

Although no cars were in the driveway and no one appeared to be home, Church knocked on the front door. He figured that Ronnie had already returned to Camp Lejeune, but he still hoped to catch Kimberly at home. He waited a few minutes, then drove next door to Kimberly's parents', James and Judy Stump's, house.

Judy Stump answered the door. She was a petite woman with short-cropped, bright red hair and glasses too big for her small, sincere face. After Church introduced himself, she openly invited him in, confirming her warm nature.

"I was wondering if Kimberly was around?" he asked.

"Yes, as a matter of fact, she is. She's in the den. Come this way."

The den was an off-set from the kitchen, wood-paneled, comfortable. Kimberly was sitting on the floor with several open catalogs spread out in front of her. She pushed the catalogs aside and stood.

Kimberly was a young woman, maybe early twenties, if that. Her face was round and open and filled with that sparkling wonder so often seen in a child. Her hair was blonde, darker at the roots, and fell in tight curls below her shoulders. She barely looked old enough to drive, thought Church, let alone be someone's wife.

"Sorry for the mess," Judy apologized and laughed. "We're trying to get some Christmas gifts ordered. Can I get you something to drink?"

"No, thank you. I'm fine. I won't be long. I just need to ask Kimberly a few questions."

Kimberly glanced at her mother, then looked back at Church and smiled tentatively. "Sure. Anything I can do to help." Her voice was high-pitched, like a little girl's.

"Have a seat, Detective Church. If you can find one." Judy chuckled as she cleared a stack of catalogs from a chair.

Church smiled and sat in the offered chair. "I assume your husband has returned to Camp Lejeune?" He had directed the question to Kimberly, but Judy was quick to answer.

"Yes, he had to get back. He had already extended his leave."

Church looked directly at Kimberly and asked, "When did he return?"

"He left Sunday afternoon. He had to be back by Monday morning."

"You said he had already extended his leave. You mean for the funeral?"

"Well, see, he was supposed to go back last Tuesday, but because of what happened, he stayed over a while. You know, with the funeral and all. But he got permission." She bobbed her head quickly as if pointing out to Church that her husband was a dutiful Marine.

"How long had he been in Greensboro?"

"He got in that Friday night. The Friday before—you know—the Friday before Patricia died."

"Was this just a visit?"

"No," she said and laughed. "He was supposed to work on the underpinning on our house. We just live next door." She waved her hand in the general direction of the new mobile home.

Underpinning, or *skirting* as it is sometimes called, hangs from the bottom of a trailer to the ground, suspended from a track that runs along the edge of the home. It is designed to cover the underbelly of the trailer, giving it a more finished look.

"Did he get the underpinning finished?" Church asked casually, smiling.

Kimberly grinned and rolled her eyes. "No. He got started on it, though. He at least got the track up."

"And he started on it that weekend?"

"No, he didn't actually get started on it until Monday. We had a bunch of errands and things to do that weekend."

"Do you know about what time he started on it that Monday?"

"Oh, it was sometime that afternoon, I think. He had to go get it first."

"The underpinning?"

She nodded. "Yeah. He had to go out to the mobile-home supply place and get it. Actually, he had gotten the wrong kind that weekend and had to exchange it. But he got an early start. He was up and gone before I left for work."

"What time was this?"

"I guess he left around seven. He had to borrow a truck from Ted before he could pick the underpinning up."

"So he went to Ted's house that morning?"

"I'm not sure if the truck was at the house or at Lyles'. He took the truck back to Lyles', though."

"What time was that, do you know?"

She shrugged. "I think it was around three o'clock. He called me while he was out there."

"He called you from Lyles'?"

She nodded.

So not only was Ronnie Kimble in Greensboro the day Patricia died, he was with Ted only hours before her death.

"Do you know what time he got home?"

"He was home when I got home. About five-thirty. Him and my daddy were working on the track."

"And what time did your daddy get home?"

Kimberly looked to her mother for the answer. "It was about five," Judy said.

"And Ronnie already had most of the track up?"

Kimberly and Judy both smiled. "No," Judy answered. "James had to help him with it."

CHAPTER NINETEEN

"So Ronnie was at Lyles' at 3:00, then back home at 5:00," DeBerry said.

Church nodded. "Yep. According to his wife, anyway."

The pair left Lt. Bryant's office. As they rounded the corner of the secretary's area, DeBerry lightly gnawed on his bottom lip, thinking hard about the new information. If this were true, there was a two-hour period when Ronnie was unaccounted for. Was it just a coincidence that those were the very hours during which, most likely, Patricia was killed? "Let's go ahead and get Charles Oliver in here and see if he can confirm Ronnie was there at 3:00."

"Jim," the secretary called, "there's a lady here to see you."

"Tell her I'll be with her in a few minutes."

"It's about Kimble."

Church and DeBerry stopped. The secretary motioned over her shoulder.

The young woman was sitting in one of the wooden

chairs, wiping her flushed cheeks with a crumpled tissue. Church recognized her from the funeral home. She had been one of the last to leave and had joined the family outside when they released the balloons.

"Hi," Church said as he approached the young woman. "I'm Detective Church. You wanted to see someone regarding Patricia Kimble?"

The young woman nodded and stood. "I'm Linda Cheek. I'm a friend . . . I was a friend of Patricia's."

"Why don't you come on back and we'll talk."

She sniffled, then stuffed the tissue into her purse and followed the detectives down the hallway.

Church motioned Linda to the chair in front of his desk. "You said you were a friend of Patricia's?"

"Yes. We were in the same Sunday school class."

"Then I assume you also know Ted?"

She glanced away and took a deep, silent breath to stop herself from crying. "Yes. That's what I wanted to talk to you about." She looked back at Church with a strong, determined expression. "Something needs to be done about him. He's . . . well, it's just not right what all he's doing."

"What is it that he's doing?"

She took a quick breath. "He's acting like he doesn't even care that his wife was just murdered. For example, the other night our Sunday school class went out to eat for one of our member's birthday. Ted was there and showing off these elaborate plans for some dream house he plans to build. He's already had the blueprints drawn up. And then there's the expensive motorcycle. Ted bought it with the money from a love offering his father's church took up for him."

Church recalled his earlier conversation with the

young woman who had called in to the Crimestoppers line. Hadn't she said Patricia and Ted had fought over a motorcycle? Ted had wanted one but Patricia felt they couldn't afford it at the time.

Linda, ready to cry at any moment, continued. "I guess the thing that really bothers me about the whole situation, though, is he's already dating again."

"Ted?" Church asked, not so much for clarity but because he, too, found the idea of dating only ten days after your wife's murder unbelievable.

"Yes," she, nodded. "He's dating a young girl named Lynette Jones. He's even brought her to church."

"Do you know much about her?"

She shook her head. "No, not really. It's not right, I know, but we're having a real hard time opening up to her. It's not her fault, we know, but we can't help it."

"When you say *we*, who are you referring to?"

"Our Sunday school class. She seems like a nice enough girl, but we . . . we just can't . . ."

DeBerry handed her a tissue, as she no longer fought the urge to cry.

"I know it's no crime to date," Linda said after a moment. "But it's like he doesn't even respect Patricia's memory."

Later, Church poked his head into DeBerry's office. "Oliver's coming in around five-thirty."

"Good. Let me know when he gets here. I'll sit in on it with you."

Church leaned against the door frame. "Can you believe he's already dating again?"

DeBerry leaned back in his chair and gnawed on the end of his pen. He shrugged. "It's kind of shallow. But unless he was dating her before Patricia's murder, it really has no bearing on the case."

"Well, to me, it shows he didn't give a damn about Patricia."

"I agree with you. But we're not a jury." He cocked his eyebrows and softly smiled.

Church stepped into the office and sat down. "What about the motorcycle? And the dream house? More than likely, he thinks he's going to pay for that house with Patricia's life insurance."

DeBerry nodded. "Probably. But it's really not for us, or anyone, to say how he spends that money. People mourn in different ways."

Church shook his head. "It ain't right."

"No, in our opinion, it's not. But the truth is, Jim, the guy's got about as much class as a slug, but we can't arrest him for it. Although it probably should be in some instances, lack of class isn't a criminal offense." DeBerry leaned in and propped his elbows on his cluttered desk. "Look, I sympathize with everyone that has come in or called regarding Patricia, but truthfully, all they've offered so far is insights into Kimble's character. That's important, but it's not going to get him arrested. And it sure won't bring a conviction."

Church sighed. He knew everything DeBerry was saying was true. So far, the only concrete evidence they had was a forged life insurance application. And that alone wasn't enough.

"Don't let it get to you, Jim," DeBerry said. "You're not doing Patricia Kimble any good if you do."

"Speaking of Patricia Kimble," Ann Mauney said as she entered the small office. She tossed a bound report on DeBerry's desk and plopped in the chair beside Church. "Got yourself a good one there, Church."

Ann Mauney was a sworn officer with the North Carolina Department of Insurance. She had the power and authority to arrest. Although she wasn't one to throw her weight around or misuse her badge, Mauney found great pleasure in arresting shady insurance salesmen who preyed on the elderly. She had seen one too many old folks, good folks, victimized by bogus policies.

Although Mauney could dress the part of the female—power-suit, complete with elegant jewelry, heels, and expensive makeup—she felt much more comfortable back on the family farm in her sweatshirt and jeans. But whether she was wearing a designer dress or dressed down, Mauney could hold her own with any high-heeled executives or their starch-shirted male counterparts.

"That's just a preliminary," Mauney said, cocking her head in DeBerry's direction, referring to the five-inch report. "You know he's already calling, wanting to know when he can collect."

"He can't, can he?" Church asked.

"The one Patricia had through work will pay out, but the big one won't. There never was a policy. All he had was an application. And it was *definitely* forged."

"What about this homeowner's policy?" DeBerry asked as he studied the report.

"That's almost a joke. He claimed $270,000 on $2,000 worth of fire damage and fifty grand on structural damage. He only upped the amount of the damage by what—two hundred grand? Guy's got some nerve."

"What about the breaking-and-entering claims, and the car claims I told you about?" Church asked.

"Still working on 'em but you can definitely see an escalating pattern. Starts with a little car damage, moves on to burglaries, and then—God forbid—his wife's life insurance."

He just kept wanting more, Church thought. He tallied how many of Patricia's friends had expressed just that.

DeBerry furrowed his brow, then looked up from the report at Mauney. "The homeowner's policy was going to be canceled?"

She nodded. "Yep. October 31. Substantial losses."

"Did Ted know this?"

"If he opens his mail, he did. He was sent a letter on October 4."

DeBerry looked back down at the report, then asked, "What's this about rent?"

Mauney laughed. "That's a good one. Teddy Boy asked for sixteen grand to cover his living expenses while he's *displaced*. Says he deserves accommodations equal to what he's accustomed to—three bedrooms, two baths. Supposedly, he's going to rent his parents' house while they move into a single-wide mobile home at the back of their property."

"What?" DeBerry and Church asked in unison.

Mauney grinned and stood. "Yep, mommy and daddy are giving up their nice three-bedroom home and moving into a trailer. The insurance company has already cut daddy a $16,000 dollar check to cover sonny's rent. You've got enough right there to arrest him for insurance fraud."

DeBerry closed the report and leaned back in his chair. "No offense to your department, but I don't want to go that route just yet."

"No offense taken." Mauney mock-saluted the sergeant and turned to leave, then turned back. "Oh, I've got a court order in to open Patricia's safe-deposit box. I'll let you know the outcome."

DeBerry watched her leave, then asked Church, "Ted hasn't come in for an interview yet, has he?"

Church shook his head. "Says he's too busy. With the funeral and all." He raised his eyebrows to match the mocking tone of his voice.

"Too busy to help find his wife's murderer. Well, then, I think it's time we pay him a visit. I'd like to hear what he has to say about this application."

Church looked at his watch. "Want to do it now? We've got a little while before Oliver comes in."

"Sure." DeBerry stood and grabbed his coat. "I don't mind taking a ride out to Lyles' Building Supplies. I'm in the market for a doghouse, anyway."

"When did you get a dog?"

"I didn't. But Kimble don't know that."

CHAPTER TWENTY

No matter what time of day, Greensboro's Lee Street was always busy. The four lanes moved at a stop-and-go pace. Stoplights at each block made matters worse. DeBerry wove his Ford Taurus around a slow-moving city bus and accelerated to make the next light. Although Lyles' Building Supplies, located on Lee Street, was only a few miles from downtown Greensboro and their office, DeBerry felt as if he could have already driven two hundred miles to the beach.

"What did Ronnie have to say when you called him at Camp Lejeune?" he asked Church.

"Oh, he boo-hooed. It was such a tragedy. He didn't know why anyone would ever want to hurt Patricia."

"What did he say about being in Greensboro that day?"

"Said he took an extra day's leave to finish underpinning the trailer. Said his wife was getting kind of ill with him because it wasn't finished yet. He's a chatty thing when he gets to talking—you can't shut him up."

DeBerry lit a cigarette and cracked the window. "Did you ask him why if his wife was getting ill with him, he waited until late afternoon to get started on it?"

"I don't think he knew what he was doing. He had to wait on his daddy-in-law to help him."

DeBerry pulled into the gravel parking lot of Lyles' and parked near the front of the building.

The building itself was a barn-shaped warehouse. The yard was overflowing with clumsily stacked lumber and plywood. In years past, when Gary Lyles owned the business, it was a well-kept supply store. Now, it had the junky look of a salvage yard.

Ted was out in the yard to the side of the building. Crouching, he meticulously wiped the gas tank of a blue-and-white Suzuki 1100, although the motorcycle's new shine already glared against the blazing sunlight. He stood as DeBerry and Church approached.

"Nice toy," DeBerry said, lifting his sunglasses to get a better look at the cycle.

"Like it?" Ted stuffed the rag that he had been using into his back pocket. He slid his hands into the front pockets of his faded jeans and leaned proudly against his new toy. "Well, you guys got anything new to tell me?"

"Detective Church tells me you haven't been down to the office yet to help us out. We could really use your help, Ted."

Ted folded his arms across his chest and kicked

lightly at the gravel. "I've been kind of busy. With the funeral and the business, and all."

DeBerry slowly nodded. "Well, it would really help us out a great deal if you'd come down and talk with us."

"Aren't we talking now?"

"Ted, aren't you interested in finding your wife's murderer?" Church asked.

"That's your job."

DeBerry stubbed his cigarette into the ground and lowered his sunglasses. "And we're pretty good at our jobs, too. Sooner or later, we usually get our man."

Ted eyed the sergeant and slowly nodded. "I'm glad."

"We just want you to know we're working day and night to find out who killed your wife. And bring them to justice."

Ted glared at DeBerry. "I appreciate that."

"Why didn't you let us know your brother was in town the day your wife was killed?" DeBerry asked.

"Because I knew my brother didn't have anything to do with it. I didn't want to get him involved." There was no hesitation in his answer. No surprise the question had even been asked.

"How do you know who was involved and who wasn't?" Church asked.

"Because I know my brother." He stared at Church hard.

DeBerry nodded. "Well, like you said, that's our job to decide who's involved and who isn't."

Ted shrugged. "Well, I can tell you, my brother wasn't involved."

"Okay. Can you tell us who signed this insurance application?"

Church held out the piece of paper for Ted's review. He quickly glanced at it, then stared at DeBerry.

"Patricia's name is on it," he said and shrugged again.

"But that's not Patricia's handwriting," Church said. "Do you know whose it is?"

Ted stared at the paper.

"You know who signed it, Ted?" DeBerry asked.

After a moment, Ted finally answered. "Yeah, I signed it." His words flowed with inflated arrogance.

"Want to tell us why?" DeBerry asked.

He sighed and looked away. "Patricia had a bad day at work. I didn't want to bother her with it."

"Is this the one you told us about the night at the church, the one you said you canceled?"

"Yeah, that's it. I signed it because she came home from work one day in a bad mood. One of the tenants at the apartments was giving her a hard time. The guy at the insurance company needed it the next day, and I didn't want to bother her anymore, so I just signed it."

"And then you canceled it?"

Ted nodded.

"You called the insurance agent and canceled it?"

He nodded again.

"How could you cancel it if the policy was never written?" DeBerry asked. He lit another cigarette.

"I didn't say I canceled the policy—I canceled the application."

"The day after you signed it?" Church asked.

"Probably not the very next day, but shortly after."

"So let me get this straight," DeBerry said. "You signed the application then called the agent to cancel it?"

"That's right."

"Then why did you call him two days after your wife's death to collect?"

Ted laughed a quick, sharp laugh. "You guys are acting like I'm a suspect."

"We're just asking you some questions, Ted," Church said.

"Well, I don't really like the direction the questions are going in. You're acting like I'm under suspicion."

"At this point, Ted," DeBerry said, "everyone that knew Patricia is under suspicion. See, it's all just a process of elimination."

Ted shifted his glare from one detective to the other. "I think I need a lawyer."

CHAPTER TWENTY-ONE

Charles Oliver tapped his long, narrow fingers on the table and glanced from one detective to the other. He glanced at his watch. He glanced at the detectives again. He scratched at a patch of beard framing his dark chin.

"How long have you worked for Ted Kimble, Mr. Oliver?" Church asked. He took a seat at the table and opened his notepad. DeBerry closed the door to the small room and sat at the other end of the table.

"Since he's owned the business, I guess." Oliver's voice was as scratchy as his beard. His head hung low. His gaze shifted from the tabletop to each of the detectives.

"Did you also work for Mr. Lyles?"

"Yeah." He shifted in his seat. He stopped tapping his fingers and began popping his swollen knuckles. Pale patches of faded skin scarred his black hands.

"So you've known Ted awhile?"

"A few years."

Ted Kimble and Patricia at her bridal shower in May 1994.

In May 1994, Ted and Patricia were married at Monnett Road Baptist Church, where Ted's father was pastor. *Lloyd's Photography*

Patricia Blakley on her wedding day with her parents, Sheila and Richard. *Lloyd's Photography*

Patricia's wedding portrait, May 1994. *Lloyd's Photography*

Gary Lyles, *left*, and Ted Kimble. Gary had known Ted from the time Ted was a child and thought of him as a son. Gary was devastated to learn he was one of the witnesses on Ted's hit list.

Lyles' Building Supply, in Greensboro, N.C., where Ted had worked for eight years, before purchasing the business in 1993. Gary Lyles had promised to sell the business to Ted once he was married and settled down. *Guilford County Sheriff's Department Photo*

October 9, 1995. Pleasant Garden firemen and investigators for the Guilford County Sheriff's Dept. at the Kimble residence the night of the fire. *Guilford County Sheriff's Department photo*

In remembrance of Patricia, friends left flowers and balloons at the burned-out home, where her body was discovered.

Detective Sergeant David DeBerry, of the Guilford County Sheriff's Department Major Crimes unit, said of the investigation, "We had good teamwork on the case throughout the entire department."

S.B.I. Special Agent Harold Pendergrass, *left*, and Detective Jim Church, outside the Guilford County Sheriff's Department in Greensboro, N.C. Church said, "It was a case of a lifetime. I hope to never have another one like it."

Monnet Road Baptist Church, where Ted and Ronnie's father was pastor. Support for the Reverend and his sons dwindled following Ronnie's conviction. The Reverend Kimble resigned from the church in July 1999.

April 1, 1997. At Lyles' Building Supply, Detective Sgt. David DeBerry, *right*, shows Sheriff BJ Barnes one of several stacks of lumber believed to have been stolen.

Guilford County Sheriff's Department photo

March 1999. Ted Kimble being led into the Guilford County Courthouse for his sentencing hearing. He holds a letter he wrote to the judge, requesting a reversal of his earlier plea arrangement. *Jerry Wolford*

September 1998. Ronnie Kimble, being led into the Guilford County Courthouse, where he stood trial for first-degree murder. *Jerry Wolford*

September 1998. Ronnie Kimble, as the jury announced its verdict in his murder trial.
Jerry Wolford

March 1999. Ted Kimble at his sentencing hearing at the Guilford County Courthouse.
Jerry Wolford

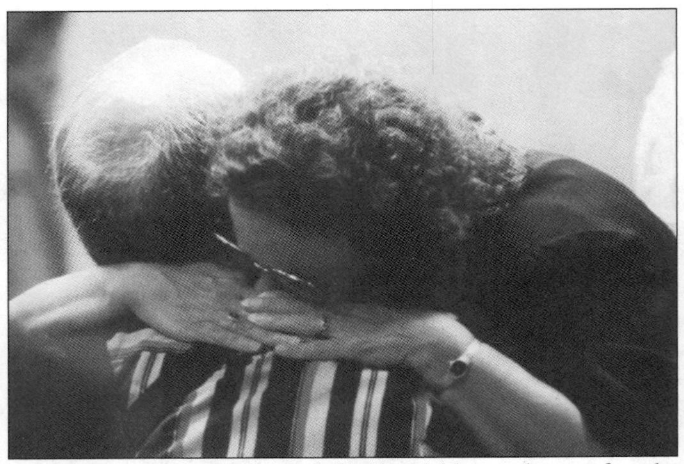

September 1998. Richard and Sheila Blakley embrace after the jury finds Ronnie Kimble guilty of murder in the death of their daughter, Patricia.
Jerry Wolford

"Did you know Patricia?"

Oliver shrugged. "I'd see her when she came out to the store."

"Did you ever talk to her?"

"We'd say hello."

"Do you know Ted's brother, Ronnie?"

He leaned back and slumped down in the wooden chair, his eyes cast downward. "Yeah, I know him."

"Do you know him well?"

"I'd see him out at the store some, that's it."

"Do you remember seeing him out at the store the day Patricia died?"

Oliver shrugged and leaned forward. Again, he worked his fingers against the table in a rapid rhythm.

"Does that mean you don't remember or you didn't see him?"

"He might have been there."

"I'm going to get a cup of coffee," DeBerry said as he stood. "You want a soda, Charles?"

Oliver glanced up at the sergeant and half nodded.

DeBerry left and returned a moment later. He tossed a canned drink to Oliver, then retook his seat. He thumped out a cigarette and lit it. "You smoke?"

Oliver nodded as he popped open the drink and took a sip. DeBerry rolled a Kool across the table, then slid Oliver his lighter.

"Who builds those doghouses you got out there at the store?" DeBerry asked, taking a sip of his coffee.

"I build most of 'em."

"You sell a lot of them?"

Oliver nodded. "Especially the cedar ones."

"People like that smell, huh?"

"Well, cedar cuts down on the fleas."

"I'll have to remember that." DeBerry stored the information in his "useless information that could come in handy" mental file cabinet and settled comfortably into the chair. "So you don't remember if Ronnie was out at the store that day?"

"He was there for a little while, off and on."

"So he was there more than once?"

"Seems like it, yeah."

"Do you remember what time it was when you last saw him?"

Oliver glanced up at the ceiling. "It was a little after three o'clock."

"Are you positive on that?" Church asked.

"Yeah, cause he was leaving just as I was getting back from lunch."

"And you're sure it was a little after three?"

"Yeah, cause I was running late getting back. I had car trouble while I was out and looked at the clock as soon as I got back."

"What clock?"

"The clock in the store. There's a big clock on the front wall."

"And Ronnie was leaving as you got back?"

Oliver nodded. "It might have been around three-fifteen, but not much after that."

"What was he doing there, do you know?"

Oliver shook his head. "He was talking to Ted. That's all I know."

Church glanced at DeBerry. Where Ronnie was concerned, they had a key part of the time frame confirmed. Now they needed to confirm one other part—what time he arrived home.

. . .

Church drove along Monnett Road carefully. It was well after dark. The darkness made the winding road difficult to navigate.

The darkness also made it difficult to read the few and far-between addresses. As he rounded a curve, the light from the sign of Monnett Road Baptist Church glowed like a beacon. It reminded Church that he was close to his destination, Ronnie's in-laws', James and Judy Stump's house.

Once he found the house, he pulled into the familiar driveway. James Stump met him at the front door. Church had called ahead, and Stump greeted him eagerly. "It's a pleasure to meet you," Stump said as he invited Church into his home. "I'm sorry it's under these circumstances, but we're willing to help all we can."

"Thank you, Mr. Stump. I appreciate your cooperation."

"Well, like I said, anything we can do to help. Why don't we go into the kitchen? We'll probably be more comfortable there."

Judy Stump was at the stove overseeing a pot of homemade vegetable stew. She smiled softly as her husband and Church moved to the kitchen table. The pleasant aroma wafting through the room triggered Church's hunger, reminding him that he had once again missed lunch.

"Kimberly's not here right now," James said as he sat down at the table. "She'll probably be over in a little bit, though."

"Oh, that's okay. It was you I actually wanted to

talk with tonight." Church sat down across from Stump at the table.

"Well, I don't know exactly how we can help, but we're willing to do whatever it takes."

"I wanted to talk to you a little about the day Patricia was killed. Kimberly told me on my first visit that you had helped Ronnie that evening put up some underpinning?"

"Well, we didn't actually get the underpinning up, but we did get the tracking finished."

"About what time did you finish the tracking?" Church asked.

"Oh, I guess it was around six o'clock. We finished up and then got cleaned up for dinner."

"What time did you get started on it, do you remember?"

"I went over there as soon as I got home from work. I usually get home around four forty-five, five o'clock."

"Do you remember, on that particular day, if it was quarter till or five o'clock?"

"Umm . . . seems like it was closer to five. We didn't get a whole lot done before we stopped for dinner."

"How was Ronnie acting that day?"

Stump looked at Church, his eyes full of questions. "He was . . . Ronnie."

Church took Stump's expression into consideration. He didn't want to alarm the man into a defensive mode. "You've known Ronnie a long time?"

Stump smiled and shook his head. "Oh, gosh . . . we've known him since he was about ten, twelve years old. We're members of his father's church, so you could say we've watched the kid grow up."

"And how long have he and Kimberly been married?"

"Little over a year, I guess."

"So Ronnie was already in the military when they got married?"

"Oh, yeah. That was one of the reasons we tried to persuade them to wait."

"You mean wait to get married?"

Stump nodded.

"Don't get us wrong, Detective Church," Judy interjected, "we think the world of Ronnie. It was just that they were so young, and he still had a while in the military."

"Judy's right," Stump said. "It's not that we don't like Ronnie, it's just that we know how hard it is to make a marriage work these days and we didn't want them starting out under a hardship. But as it turns out, we couldn't have asked for a better husband for our daughter."

Church had his doubts but kept them to himself. "You said the military was one of the reasons you tried to discourage the marriage. Were there other reasons?"

The Stumps looked at one another. Judy turned back to the stove; her husband looked at Church and sighed. "Don't get us wrong, Detective Church," he said. "We think the world of Ronnie. He's a good boy. We were just a little concerned about his . . . problems."

"What type of problems?"

Stumped sighed again and shifted in his chair. "Ronnie had a difficult childhood. We were a little concerned some of those *difficulties* might carry over."

"What kind of difficulties?"

"Well, Ronnie's a little slow about some things. He was always in the slower classes in school. He has trouble staying focused, concentrating. But he's one of the friendliest boys you'll ever meet. He's probably a little too friendly." Stump slightly chuckled, then continued. "He just wants people to love him. He didn't get a lot of affection at home when he was younger, and he sometimes goes overboard wanting people to like him."

Church waited a moment, then returned to the day Patricia died. "Mr. Stump, when you got home that day, the day Patricia died, how much of the tracking did Ronnie have up?"

Stump smiled. It was a sad smile. "Not much. I think he was waiting on me to help."

Either that, Church thought, or perhaps Ronnie had just gotten home himself.

CHAPTER TWENTY-TWO

The next morning DeBerry headed for Camp Lejeune. The base occupied over 150,000 prime acres in Jacksonville, North Carolina, along the state's coast. Camp Lejeune was home to some 47,000 Marines and sailors.

DeBerry gazed at the sprawling military base from a spotless window in the chaplain's office where Ronnie worked. Towering pine trees lined the sandy landscape. State-of-the-art buildings boasted manicured hedges. The scent of pine and salty air mingled, much to DeBerry's delight. He wished he'd brought his fishing rods. It didn't matter, though. It was to be a one-day trip, and he doubted he'd have time. From Camp Lejeune, he'd drive the coast to Long Beach to meet with Gary and Rose Lyles, the former owners of Lyles' Building Supplies.

He waited patiently in the chaplain's office for Ronnie, but after the four-hour drive, he was tired of sitting and moved casually from window to window.

"Ronnie should be back any minute," the secretary

said. "Actually, he should have already been back. He's just running an errand. Can I get you something to drink while you wait?"

"No, thank you. I'm fine," DeBerry said and smiled politely.

"Is this about his sister-in-law?"

DeBerry strolled to the next window. "Has Ronnie said much about her death?"

"Oh, he was pretty upset. I'd say he was devastated."

"Were they very close?"

She lifted her shoulders in a half-shrug. "I don't really know. Judging from his reaction, I'd say so, though."

The main door jerked open and Ronnie breezed in. The door slammed hard behind him as he moved hurriedly through the office, a wide smile on his face.

"Ah—Ronnie," the secretary said, "you have a visitor." She motioned her head toward DeBerry.

DeBerry smiled and strolled toward the Marine, his hand proffered. "Hi," he said, "Detective Sergeant David DeBerry, Guilford County Sheriff's Department."

Ronnie's smile sank into a twitching frown as he accepted the sergeant's hand.

"Can I speak with you for a minute, Ronnie?"

"Um . . . sure." He placed his sweaty hands on his hips and stared at DeBerry, a hesitant smile slowly returning. "Shoot." They stared at each other for a moment, then Ronnie laughed. "Not a very smart thing to say to a cop!"

DeBerry faked a laugh. "We only shoot when necessary."

"Always ready, though. Just like us Marines."

And the Boy Scouts, DeBerry thought. Wasn't it the Boy Scout motto—always be ready? Or prepared? Something like that. He wasn't sure. He was never a Boy Scout.

"Is there somewhere more private that we can talk?" DeBerry asked. He glanced down the hallway at the line of offices.

"Oh. Um . . . we can go over here. To the reception area." He walked a few feet to two wooden chairs and an end table near the main door. Comfort and extended guest visits clearly weren't the idea behind the so-called reception area. Three Marines in fatigues burst through the door, laughingly raucously. Their conversation was equally loud as they passed Ronnie and DeBerry.

"There's not an office available?" DeBerry asked.

"Oh, no. Probably not at this time of day. This will be fine. We won't be bothered." Ronnie sat in one of the chairs and smiled at DeBerry as if he had just won a sweepstakes.

DeBerry relented and sat down next to him in the other chair. It wasn't the ideal place to conduct an interview of any kind, but he wanted Ronnie comfortable.

"So, what did you want to talk to me about?" Ronnie asked with a puzzling innocence.

"Your sister-in-law's murder."

"Oh. That." Ronnie looked down at the floor, staring at his boots. His breath quickened, keeping rhythm with his tapping feet.

As DeBerry ran through a series of basic questions, Ronnie became more agitated, and emotional.

"What did you do after you exchanged the underpinning?" DeBerry asked the question three times and each time was met with the same gasping answer.

"I just don't understand why anyone would want to hurt Patricia," Ronnie sobbed, his face a landscape of emotion.

DeBerry tried again. "Ronnie, where did you go after you left the mobile-home supply store?"

"I stopped and got gas. I had to fill the truck back up before I took it back to Ted."

"But what did you do the rest of the afternoon?"

"I got a receipt."

DeBerry stared at him a moment. "A receipt?"

"Yeah, I got a receipt for the gas. I left it in the truck." He glanced at DeBerry, then quickly looked away.

Is he telling me to look in the truck? DeBerry wondered. Something wasn't right about this boy.

"Did you leave anything else in the truck, Ronnie?"

He quickly shook his head. "Just the receipt."

"And what time was it you stopped and got gas?"

"Around lunchtime. Maybe one o'clock."

Then why the big deal over a receipt? The only thing it would prove was that he had indeed gotten gas.

A group of Marines bumped through the main door, loudly greeting others congregated a few feet away. Ronnie watched them a moment, then stared back down at his tapping feet.

"Okay, so you went and got gas," DeBerry said, trying to reel in Ronnie's wandering attention. "Then what did you do the rest of the afternoon?"

"I went home and unloaded the underpinning. It would have been stupid of me to take the truck back to Ted with the underpinning still on it. I wouldn't have had any way of getting it back down to my house. Don't you think it would have been stupid?"

DeBerry slowly nodded. "Yeah, that was probably a smart thing to do. Did you take the truck back to Ted's house or out to Lyles'?"

"Pardon?" Ronnie said, now grinning at the conversation taking place a few feet away.

"I asked if you took the truck back to Ted's house or out to Lyles'."

"Oh. I took it out to Lyles. I had left my car there, and I wouldn't have had any way to get home if I had taken it to Ted's house. It would have been stupid of me to take it to his house. Don't you think?"

Again, DeBerry nodded. "Yeah, you're right. Good thing you think of things like that."

A satisfied smile crept across Ronnie's face. "Yeah. I mean, I guess I could have waited around until my wife got off work and had her pick me up—"

"Picked you up from where?"

"Ted's house. If I had taken the truck back there. But she didn't get off for another two hours, and it would have been stupid for me to sit around doing nothing for two hours."

"Do you remember what time you took the truck back?"

"Sometime that afternoon." Ronnie scratched at his neck. He tapped his feet. He chuckled at his fellow Marines. "I'm not sure exactly what time it was, I just know it was sometime that afternoon."

"Well, you said your wife didn't get off work for another two hours. What time does she normally get off?"

"Five." His lips began to quiver, his eyes to glisten.

"So, that would mean it was around three o'clock that you took the truck back out to Lyles'?"

"Yeah, it *was* around three," he said, excited, as if this were a totally new revelation. "I know that because when I left there I got behind a school bus, so school was out by then. Or maybe it was about to let out. I don't know if the bus was going or coming." His words were tangled in excited breaths.

"Did the bus stop to let any kids off?" DeBerry asked.

Ronnie looked at DeBerry with a puzzled expression, then nodded excitedly. "Yeah, they were stopping every few blocks. So they must have been coming from the school, wouldn't you think?"

DeBerry nodded. "Yeah, I'd probably say so."

A few of the Marines tromped past and slammed the door as they left. A few more entered. Ronnie watched each movement with great interest.

"Ronnie, you said you left Lyles' around three o'clock. Where did you go after that?"

"Pardon?"

"After you left Lyles', where did you go?"

More Marines left; more came in.

Ronnie took a deep breath and began to cry again. "I just don't understand why anyone would want to hurt Patricia," he sputtered.

"Ronnie, where did you go when you left Lyles'?" DeBerry tried again.

"She was so sweet. Why would anyone want to hurt her?" he wailed. The group of Marines glanced over at the scene.

"Ronnie, do you want to go somewhere private?" DeBerry asked quietly.

Sternly, Ronnie shook his head. All of a sudden, he sprang from the chair. "I've got to get back to work."

DeBerry stood. "Ronnie, wait . . ."

"Naw, I better get back." Ronnie moved away from DeBerry and headed toward the hallway of offices. "It's been nice talking to you, though."

DeBerry glanced around at the other Marines. For once, they were quiet. Well, this sure went nowhere fast, he thought. But if nothing else, DeBerry's gut feeling told him Ronnie Kimble knew more about Patricia's death than he was ready to admit.

Because I know my brother didn't have anything to do with it. DeBerry ran the comment Ted had made over and over again in his head. As he left Camp Lejeune and drove south along Highway 17 to Long Beach, he replayed the conversation he and Church had with Ted. He also replayed the conversation he just had with Ronnie. There was definitely something odd about both exchanges. He didn't really feel either of the brothers was outright lying, but perhaps half-truths covered the hidden truth.

Highway 17 skirted the Carolina coastline, bordered by summer-exhausted beach towns and quaint seaports. To DeBerry's dismay, the parking lots were full and the boat docks were empty. He gazed out over the ocean and imagined the roll of the waves and that sweet hum of a fishing line being tested by a trophy-sized mackerel. DeBerry had hoped to get his own boat in the water by fall. Having spent the last several months rebuilding it from the hull up, he was eager to take it out for its maiden voyage. But another fall was slowly slipping away. Maybe one day he'd leave all the murders and rapes and robberies behind.

As he drove into Long Beach, he passed clusters of oceanfront homes, each tagged with wooden signs proclaiming nautical names like Captain's Quarters and Sea Treasure. The Lyles' home was on a short side street a block from the shore. DeBerry pulled into the driveway and parked outside the chain-link gate.

"Good to see you again, Sergeant DeBerry," Gary Lyles said as he stepped onto the front porch. "Didn't have any trouble finding it, did you?"

"Came right to it." DeBerry patted the head of a large dog, a boxer, which had come to either eat him or greet him. He hoped it was the latter.

"She won't hurt you," Lyles said and called the dog back. "She's all bark, very little bite."

DeBerry laughed and scratched the dog behind its ears. She soon lopped over to the porch and sidled beside Lyles.

"So where do we stand in the investigation?" Lyles asked as he escorted DeBerry into the house.

"We're getting there. Slowly, but it's coming together."

Lyles introduced his wife to the sergeant, and the trio made themselves comfortable in the small living room. It was a cozy room with simple furniture. Framed portraits of grandchildren were proudly displayed on the wide sill of a bay window.

"It's still so hard to believe," Rose Lyles said. Her voice was delicate, as soft as cotton.

"That it is," Gary said. He pushed back the worn arms of a comfortable recliner and rested his feet.

"Gary, from what Detective Church told me," DeBerry said, "you have a rather close relationship with Ted."

Lyles nodded firmly. "Yes. The boy's like a son to me. We thought of them both, Ted and Patricia, as if they were our own." He reached over and took Rose's hand.

"We've kind of run into a brick wall with Ted, Gary. We were hoping you might be able to help."

Lyles leaned forward, a look of concern on his face. "What do you mean?"

"Ted isn't offering much help. He won't talk to us, and it's not making our investigation an easy one."

"What do you mean he won't talk to you?"

"We've asked him repeatedly to come down to the office and talk to us, but he's declined each time. We've offered to go out to his office, but he says he's too busy. The couple of times we have been out there, he really hasn't been much help."

Lyles stroked his mustache and frowned. "The day I came up to your office and talked to Detective Church, I left there and went straight over to the store. I told that boy he needed to get his rear-end up there and talk to you guys. And he still hasn't done it?"

DeBerry shook his head. "It's not casting a very good light on him, Gary."

Lyles stood and walked to the window. With his back to the living room, he gazed outside. "Dear God . . . I really don't want to think what I'm thinking."

Rose began to cry quietly. She pressed her hands against her chest. "Gary," she said, her soft voice barely audible, "you didn't tell them about the phone call, did you?"

Lyles turned around. "No. I didn't really think too much about it at the time. I thought Patricia was probably just . . . overreacting. I'm not so sure now."

"What phone call?" DeBerry asked.

Lyles sat back down in the recliner and softly patted Rose's hand. "You tell him, sweetheart. You're the one she talked to."

Rose rubbed her chest and took a deep breath. "The Friday before she died, Patricia called here. She wanted to talk to Gary, but he wasn't here. She was so upset, she just had to talk to someone, so the poor thing poured her heart out to me. She was so afraid. The poor thing." Tears rolled down Rose's round cheeks. "She had just found out about an insurance policy Ted had taken out on her, and the little thing was absolutely terrified. She was so scared, Sergeant DeBerry. I felt so sorry for her.

"She couldn't understand why he would do such a thing. Especially since she had told him they didn't need any more insurance. I'll never forget this as long as I live: she said, 'Rose, I'm telling you this in case anything ever happens to me—it's Ted.' "

Gary Lyles shook his head, then buried his face in his hands. He sat like that for a moment, then gazed up at DeBerry. "We didn't think too much about it at the time. I thought she was just overreacting."

"She just wanted someone to know," Rose said. "She couldn't believe this was happening to her." With that, Rose burst out crying and clutched her chest. Gary grabbed a small bottle from the end table and gave her a nitroglycerin tablet. He softly stroked her hand, waiting for her to calm down.

"Rose has a heart condition," he explained to DeBerry. "She's not in the best of health."

DeBerry gave them a minute to collect themselves.

"I'm sorry," Lyles said. "All of this is just a little hard to accept."

"Do you think Ted may have had something to do with Patricia's death?"

"I don't want to. Lord knows, I don't want to. But it's certainly beginning to look that way, isn't it?"

"Gary, given your relationship with Ted, do you think he'd talk with you?"

"You mean about his possible involvement?"

DeBerry nodded. "Yes. Do you think you could get him to talk?"

Lyles stood and slowly strolled around the room, shaking his head. "No. Ted wouldn't talk to me about something like that. See, Ted knows me—he knows, regardless of our relationship, I'm a firm believer in what's right and what's wrong. He knows, even if he were my own blood, if he were to . . . admit to something, I'd urge him to turn himself in, then I'd go straight to the authorities."

"So you don't think it would even be worth a shot?" DeBerry asked.

Lyles shook his head. "He knows me too well. If he has something to hide, I'm the last person he'd tell. I'm afraid I can't help you there, Sergeant."

CHAPTER TWENTY-THREE

The day after he returned from Camp Lejeune, DeBerry assembled his detectives in the conference room. "Bring all your notes," he said.

He flipped to a clean page on the large writing tablet and placed it on the easel. With a black marker, he dissected the page with horizontal lines, labeling each in fifteen-minute intervals. DeBerry filled in what he knew had occurred the day Patricia died.

7:00 A.M.	Ronnie leaves home; goes to Ted's to get box truck.
7:30 A.M.	Ted arrives at Lyles.
8:00 A.M.	Patricia arrives at Cinnamon Ridge.
12:00 P.M.	Ted and Patricia have lunch at Lyles.
1:00 P.M.	Ronnie stops for gas (receipt).
1:00 P.M.	Charles Oliver, employee at Lyles, leaves for lunch.
1:30 P.M.	Patricia arrives back at work.

2:00 P.M.	Oliver calls Ted at Lyles—having car problems, will be late getting back from lunch.
3:15 P.M.	Oliver arrives back at Lyles.
3:15 P.M.	Ronnie leaves Lyles.
3:25 P.M.	Ted calls Patricia at work (according to co-worker of Patricia's).
3:30 P.M.	Patricia leaves work—is seen by a friend heading north on Randleman Road (?)
4:00 P.M.	Patricia arrives home (?)
4:50 P.M.	James Stump arrives home, goes to Ronnie's to help with underpinning.
5:30 P.M.	Ted leaves Lyles, meets mother at Biscuitville, from there goes to Mrs. Winner's Chicken and Biscuits.
6:10 P.M.	Ted arrives at Precision Fabrics.
8:30 P.M.	Ted calls Reuben.
8:40 P.M.	Reuben and Kristy arrive at Brandon Station Court.
8:45 P.M.	911 call placed.

DeBerry stepped back from the easel and looked it over. "Am I leaving out anything?" he asked, turning to the detectives.

They scanned through their notes and shook their heads.

"Obviously, the most crucial time is between 3:30, when Patricia left Cinnamon Ridge, and 6:00, when she was more than likely already dead."

"Why was she heading north on Randleman Road?" Byrd asked. "Pleasant Garden's south."

DeBerry shook his head. "That we don't know."

Church had checked with FedEx, located a few miles north of the apartments, to see if perhaps she had sent or picked up a package. But they showed no receipts for Patricia Kimble, Cinnamon Ridge, or Lyles'. He had checked with Eckerd's Drug Store in the Spring Valley Shopping Center, also a few miles north, to see if Patricia, a picture buff, had dropped off or picked up film. They, too, had no tickets in Patricia's name.

"Maybe she ran to the bank?" McBride said. "Didn't she do some of her banking at Wachovia on Randleman Road?"

Again, DeBerry shook his head. "That Monday was Columbus Day. The banks were closed."

"And Patricia would have known that," Church added.

DeBerry sat on the edge of the table and stared at the timeline. "Or maybe when Ted called at 3:25, he sent her on an errand."

"What kind of errand?" McBride asked.

The sergeant slowly shook his head and gnawed on his bottom lip, deep in thought. "A useless errand. Just something to stall her." He glanced over his shoulder at the detectives. "Anything to give Ronnie time to get down to the house."

Later that morning, Ann Mauney called Church.

"We opened Patricia's safe-deposit box," she said. "I'll fax you a copy of the item list."

"Anything interesting in it?"

"Nah—just regular stuff. Insurance policies, birth certificates, their marriage certificate from Danville, Virginia, stuff like that."

Church sat up in his chair. "Whoa—wait a minute! Their marriage certificate from where?"

"Danville, Virginia. I think. Hold on a minute." The sound of shuffling papers carried through the phone line, then Mauney returned. "Yeah, says right here—Danville."

"What's the date on that?"

"Um . . . December 1993. Why?"

"That's not when they were married," Church said. He was a stickler for dates, and this was the first time he'd heard mention of a December wedding. "They were married May 7, 1994. At Monnett Road Baptist Church. Reverend Kimble married them."

"Well, the good reverend didn't marry them in Virginia, but according to this certificate, he witnessed it."

As soon as Church hung up with Mauney, he headed for United Parcel Service, where Reuben Blakley worked. Reuben was on the docks loading one of the trucks when Church arrived.

"Can I talk to you a minute, Reuben?" Church asked, raising his voice to be heard above the conveyor belts.

"Yeah, sure. Let me tell my supervisor." He disappeared into an office, then returned a moment later. "We can walk outside if you want to. It's probably quieter."

As they walked away from the loading dock, the noise died down and settled into the low hum of machinery. They walked to a grassy knoll on the other side of the parking lot and sat down at a picnic table.

"Agent Mauney just told me what she found in Patricia's safe-deposit box. About a marriage certificate."

Reuben half-frowned and looked away. "Oh, that."

"Did you know about it?"

Reuben shook his head. "No, we just found out a few days ago. Mama knew. She's the one that told us."

"Your mother knew they were married earlier?"

"Yeah, but she didn't know about it either until maybe a few months ago. Patricia told her."

"Did she give your mother any kind of explanation?"

"She said it was so they could travel as man and wife, but that don't really make any sense. They had traveled before together, and the church wedding wasn't but a couple months off. I think it was for tax purposes. Gary Lyles was trying to line everything up to sell Ted the business and . . ." He shrugged his shoulders. "Who knows?"

"Who knew about this marriage?"

"Just them—Ted and Patricia, and his parents. They went with them."

Church tried to make sense of the information but was coming up empty. Why would Ted's father—a man of God—be part of the deception, when the one person Patricia was closest to, her own mother, was kept in the dark?

"Reuben, I know Patricia had a keen business sense

about her, but do you think the tax reasons were her idea?"

Reuben was quick to shake his head. "No. She wanted the fairytale too much. She wanted the big church wedding and the bridesmaids and dresses and all that. She wanted the white-picket fence."

"Do you think it was Ted's idea?"

Reuben laughed. His was a small laugh, filled with sadness. "Yeah. I'm pretty certain it was his idea. There's no telling what Ted can talk a person into."

CHAPTER TWENTY-FOUR

Saturday, September 9, 1995

"Anyone want anything else?" Patricia asked as she covered the pot of baked beans. "Last call." She laughed.

The small crowd of friends from Sunday school responded with various moans and groans associated with overstuffed bellies and cookouts. They were scattered about Patricia and Ted's backyard, lounging in folding chairs. The late evening air carried the scent of spent charcoal, hamburgers, and hot dogs as the cookout wound down.

"Everything was wonderful, as usual," Linda Cheek said.

The others agreed and praised Patricia's abilities as a hostess. She loved playing hostess. She reveled in seeing others enjoy themselves. Today, though, her heart wasn't really into it. She hoped no one noticed. She tried to laugh and smile as expected.

"Well, if everyone's through," she said, "I'm going

to start getting this stuff back in the house before it gets dark."

"Here, let me help." Linda pulled herself up from a lounge chair and filled her arms with bottles of condiments. The other women pitched in and soon cleared the picnic table while the men walked around to the carport to get a look at Ted's new boat.

In the kitchen, Kristy filled the sink with warm, soapy water. "You want to keep the silverware?" she asked.

Patricia laughed. "You know better than to ask. That silverware has seen us through a lot of cookouts." Although it was plastic, Patricia didn't see any need to throw it away when it could simply be washed and used again. She dropped the plastic spoons into the dishwater and gave Kristy a slight grin.

"Want to put these tomatoes in a bowl?" Linda asked.

"Oh, yeah. Sure. They're under the second cabinet." Patricia tossed a couple of stray pieces of lettuce in the garbage, then wiped her hands and sighed. She was trying. Lord knows she was trying. Still, smiling hadn't been too easy lately.

Linda clapped the lid onto the bowl and gazed at Patricia. "You okay?"

Patricia didn't answer immediately but soon after smiled and nodded. "Yeah, sure. Just have a lot on my mind, I guess."

"Did Ted start his new job?"

"Yeah, he started last week. He seems to like it." She lifted her eyebrows, trying to perk up, although discussing Ted and his second job certainly wasn't the best way to do that. She still didn't understand why he felt he needed it.

Outside, the men clustered around Ted, eager to see what new toy he'd proudly display. Reuben joined in the crowd but felt a twinge of hesitation. Something wasn't quite right with Patricia. He couldn't put his finger on it, but whatever it was, he knew it centered around Ted.

"Come here, guys, let me show you this," Ted said, strolling out of the carport toward the Jeep Cherokee.

Reuben wondered what Ted had this time. It couldn't be something on the Jeep—he already had added five grand worth of options.

Ted opened the driver's side door, reached in, and removed a Glock .45. That gun wasn't new. Reuben had seen it before. But the laser sight mounted on its top was.

"Isn't this the coolest thing? Check this out." Ted handled the gun like a pro, aiming directly at the living-room window. A pencil-thin ray of red light beamed through the glass, shone past the living room, and into the kitchen.

Reuben's heart jumped as his eyes followed the trail of the beam. A small red circle glowed dead center against his sister's head.

CHAPTER TWENTY-FIVE

It was the week of Thanksgiving 1995, almost two months since Patricia's death. For Church, it had been two months of chasing down leads that lead nowhere, two months of interviewing everyone Patricia had known—sometimes twice, sometimes three times, sometimes more. Interviewing everyone except Ted.

He still had yet to talk in depth to anyone associated with the case. Except the local news media.

The day before Thanksgiving, Church hurried through the hallway and into the conference room where DeBerry, Lt. Bryant, and Sheriff Barnes were waiting. They had gotten word that Ted had requested an interview with one of the local news stations. The interview was supposed to air that evening.

Church dropped his coat in his chair and joined the others around a small television in the conference room.

It was the lead story and began with a shot of Ted in the yard at Lyles' Building Supplies. He was holding Patricia's wedding portrait. The voice-over indicated the grieving husband was offering a $20,000 reward for information leading to the arrest of his wife's killer. The money, Ted said, would come from his wife's insurance policy.

"You mean the policy that didn't exist," DeBerry added as the scene changed to a one-on-one interview between Ted and a reporter.

Ted was wearing a faded denim jacket over a flannel shirt, his face cleanly shaven. As soon as he realized the camera was rolling, his upbeat, lighthearted nature changed to that of a somber widower. "I loved my wife," he said into the camera. "We had a good marriage."

Off camera, the reporter asked Ted the purpose of the interview. Ted replied that he wanted to set the record straight. "The truth will clear me," Ted said, looking directly into the camera. "How far can they twist the truth?"

"Who is *they*?" the reporter asked.

"The Sheriff's Department. They're acting like I did it. Like I killed my wife."

"Did you?"

Ted's eyes widened as he stared at the reporter. "No. I did not kill my wife."

"The Sheriff's Department has said that you're not cooperating with them in the investigation. Is that true?"

Ted laughed. "I called them all the time. I called almost every day wanting to know where they were in the investigation. I've even given them other leads. Whether they've checked them out or not, I don't know. I just feel like they've zeroed in on me and won't even look at anyone else."

"But you haven't called them lately?"

"Would you call someone who was trying to put you in the electric chair?" He shifted his eyes downward. "I was happily married—we walked the walk. We were in church every time the doors were open. It's not their loss.

"There isn't a day that goes by that I don't think of her." His lips began to quiver, his eyes teared over. "They're not the ones who live with it. I am. I get up in the morning, and she's not there. I go to bed at night, and she's not there. No one knows what I've gone through these last two months."

"Do you have any idea who may have killed your wife?"

As quickly as the tears had begun, they stopped. Ted's gaze darted from left to right. "I have my thoughts. But whoever it was, if they don't answer for it here, they'll answer for it someday."

"You mean to you?"

Ted's eyes widened as he stared at the reporter. "No, to God. They'll answer to God one day. I'm not a violent person. I don't get mad."

"But you're mad now at the Sheriff's Department?"

"Yeah, I'm mad." He leaned forward in the chair. "Hey, buddy, I loved my wife. It's been two months since her murder, and those fools haven't done anything but come after me."

"Does the Sheriff's Department know about the reward you're offering?"

"I don't have much to say to them anymore."

"What do you hope will come out of this interview, Ted?"

"I hope somebody who knows something will

come forward. I think the money will help encourage them to do that. And then I want to be able to walk up in every one of those detectives' faces and say, *I told you so*."

The TV screen faded to black and then returned to the news anchor. As they introduced the next story, DeBerry turned the television off.

"He's telling the truth about one thing," DeBerry said. "*He* didn't kill his wife. But I'll guarantee you he knows who did." He flipped a pen on the table as he plopped down into a chair.

"He definitely had some good word choices," Bryant said. "*I* didn't kill my wife. *I* was happily married."

"*I'm* a pathological liar," DeBerry added. The men laughed. "His eye movement will tell you that."

"What about these other leads he was talking about," Barnes asked. "Have they been checked out?"

"That's all Mac and Herb's been doing these last six weeks. We've checked every name, every angle . . . they've run their asses off, and nothing's panned out. Everything keeps coming right back to Kimble."

"*Has* he called with other leads?"

DeBerry nodded. "He called once. Tried to tell us the fire on Ritter's Lake Road a few weeks ago was the same situation as his."

"How the hell does he get that?" Bryant asked. "The fire on Ritter's Lake was drug related, wasn't it?"

"Yeah, it was a deal that went south. The idiots even torched the wrong house."

"What about the insurance angle?" Barnes asked.

DeBerry retrieved his pen and gnawed the end of

it. "We've got enough to nail him on it, but I'm scared if we do, we'll lose the homicide."

Bryant agreed. "Dee's right. We stand a better chance of him messing up if he's on the outside."

"There's just not a lot to go on right now," DeBerry said. "There is no proverbial smoking gun, there are no fingerprints, there just isn't any physical evidence. Everything we've got is circumstantial."

"What does the DA's office have to say about it?" Barnes asked.

DeBerry shook his head. "It's not enough. We've got a shitload of circumstantial evidence, but it's not enough to get a conviction. We'd be lucky if we could even get an indictment."

Throughout Ted's interview and now during their conversation, Church had remained silent. DeBerry studied him carefully, eyeing the dark, half-moon circles under his eyes. The case was beginning to take its toll. DeBerry had experienced the same frustrations with other cases in his career. He knew the warning signs.

CHAPTER TWENTY-SIX

The weeks since Patricia's death were quickly sliding into months, and the holidays were passing just as quickly. Church normally looked forward to Christmas, but this year, it was just a date. A date that did nothing but remind him of how long Patricia had been dead.

"Jim," Brenda said, "come look at the carolers." She held the front door open and shivered at the rush of cold air.

Their voices lifted heavenward, filling the sparkling night with a joyous sound. Gamely, they huddled together to ward off the cold, their carol books clutched in shivering hands.

Church forced a smile as he looked out over the sea of cheerful faces. It was three days before Christmas. By this time in years past, he would have already delivered fruit baskets to the nursing homes, the eaves of his house would be strung with colorful lights, and the presents he had bought for Brenda and the kids would be wrapped and under the tree. This year, he had yet to buy the first gift. He hadn't had time, for one thing. And no matter how hard he tried, he just couldn't find the spirit.

Brenda watched her husband turn away from the carolers and retreat into the den. He had missed the last two board meetings at the Volunteer Fire Department, had even missed the last couple of fire calls. And he had nearly missed Dana's graduation ceremony, having slipped in at the last moment.

Night after night, Brenda had wakened to find him sitting on the edge of the bed, adding a name here or there to the cardboard timeline, the soft glow from the lamp on the nightstand casting a shadow across the room. Sometimes he'd talk about it. Most of the time he wouldn't. He talked occasionally about Sheila Blakley's sorrow-filled eyes. Occasionally, he would recite something his father had told him years ago—about how if someone puts their trust and faith in you, you don't let them down.

Brenda peeked into the den, then turned into the kitchen. Sometimes it was best to leave him alone.

He kicked back the footrest of the recliner and rested his feet, then slipped on a set of headphones attached to the stereo. As the sound of Mozart filtered through, Church closed his eyes. What good it would do, he didn't know. Sooner or later, he'd see those eyes again, those eyes of a heartbroken mother.

Sheila Blakley lay on her worn sofa, her knees drawn to her chest, her hands clutched under her chin. She stared at the empty spot near the picture window where last year a small Christmas tree had stood, its tiny twinkling lights reflecting against the glass.

For years after she and Richard separated, she hadn't seen the need in even putting up a Christmas tree. But Patricia had insisted. She showed up on Sheila's doorstep one Saturday morning a week before Christmas, flakes of snow clinging to her toboggan cap, her arms loaded down with boxes of decorations and a four-foot artificial tree to put them on. "You *are* going to have a Merry Christmas," she had said.

Sheila pulled her legs tighter against herself as tears rolled down her cheeks.

CHAPTER TWENTY-SEVEN

Valentine's Day, 1996

Christmas had come and gone, and a new year had been ushered in. January had brought ice storms and snow to North Carolina, that made many look forward to the warmer days of spring. Although it was only February, Church knew spring was just around the corner. Beyond that, the humid days of summer, and beyond that . . . he wondered how many days, how many months, how many seasons it would take before he could bring some amount of justice to the Blakley family.

A bone-cold wind whirled through the leaf-bare trees, echoing a mournful sound. It had been three months since Church last visited the crime scene. His need to reconnect was overwhelming. As he ducked under the yellow tape and stepped into the shell of what once was Patricia's home, his skin tingled and the hair on the back of his neck stood straight.

Roses—dozens of them, some red, some pink—filled the hole where Patricia had died. Stuffed teddy bears wearing tiny "I Love You" T-shirts—the word *love* replaced by red valentine hearts—lined the exposed floor joists. Clusters of red and silver heart-shaped Mylar balloons fluttered about. The brutal wind whipped through the broken windows, pushing the balloons into spiraling, shiny bundles.

Church walked into the skeletal hallway of two by fours and stood over the hole where Patricia had died. He stood perfectly still and listened to the eerie hum of the wind. His grandmother used to say if you got real still and listened real close, you could hear what needed to be heard. "The Lord speaks to you in all kinds of ways," she had said. "You just have to clear your mind and listen."

"I'm listening, Grandma," he said softly. "God, how I'm listening." He eased himself to the floor and leaned back against a two-by-four. He gazed at the teddy bears, the balloons, the flowers. But it was the darkened hole his gaze kept going back to. And it was Sheila Blakley's eyes he kept seeing.

And it was her anguished voice he heard in the wind. He heard her sorrowful wail as she cried her daughter's name. He heard the shrieking scream that she had emitted the night of the fire. He heard her pitiful pleas.

Church closed his eyes and prayed.

DeBerry stepped into the elevator and pressed the button for the second floor. He had been summoned to Sheriff Barnes's office where the sheriff and Lt. Bryant were waiting.

As the elevator lurched upward, DeBerry leaned

against the wall, taking advantage of the brief moment of solitude. It was late in the day, and his body felt every hour of it. Although Bryant hadn't told him the agenda, DeBerry had an idea what the meeting would entail. He wasn't looking forward to it. There was an uneasy tension brewing, but no one spoke of it. They didn't have to. They felt it.

The elevator doors opened. DeBerry stood there a moment before stepping off. Finally, he squared his shoulders and marched into the massive office.

Sheriff Barnes rose from behind an impressive oak desk and strolled around to the front of it. "Come on in, Dee, and have a seat. The lieutenant and I were just discussing the Kimble case."

"We were talking about the PI the Blakleys have hired," Bryant said.

DeBerry wasn't overly fond of private investigators, but the Blakleys' PI, Herman McCauley, had thus far proved himself trustworthy.

The Blakleys had hired McCauley around the end of January on the recommendation of Sheila's niece. He had spent twenty-two years with the Port Authority Police Department in Queens, New York, working out of the 113th precinct as a detective sergeant. With aging parents in North Carolina, McCauley retired from the force in 1993 and headed south, landing in Greensboro, where he opened his practice in 1994.

Tall, black, and handsome, McCauley had broken the "good ol' boy" network with charm and grace. In the few weeks he had worked the Kimble case, he had melded easily into the fold.

The only fault DeBerry could find with the PI wasn't even with McCauley himself. The fact that the

Blakleys had hired him meant that somewhere along the line they had lost confidence.

"Dee, we've got a problem." The sheriff leaned against the edge of his desk, hands pushed deep into his pockets. "The Blakleys are wanting to know why we haven't made an arrest yet."

DeBerry glanced at the sheriff, then at Bryant, then sighed. "We haven't made an arrest yet because all we've got is circumstantial evidence and a lot of hear-say."

"We've made cases before on circumstantial evidence," Bryant said. "Sometimes with less than we've got now."

DeBerry shook his head. "What we've got won't hold up in front of a jury. You know that, Grady. Hell, I doubt we could even get an indictment."

The sheriff returned to his seat behind his desk. "What about the insurance fraud?"

"Oh, we could make that charge, no doubt. But I'm telling you, if we arrest him on that, we're going to lose the homicide. Once he lawyers up, we'll never get anything out of him. He hasn't given us anything to begin with, but at least if he's on the outside, as a free man, odds are he'll mess up."

"And how long are we supposed to wait for him to mess up?" Barnes raised his eyebrows and leaned back in his chair. "What do we do in the meantime?"

DeBerry stared at the sheriff, then at Bryant. "We do what we've done every day since Patricia Kimble died. No one has let up on this, Sheriff."

Barnes leaned forward, clasping his hands together and propping them on his desk. "David—I wasn't implying that anyone had. All I'm saying is, we've got an upset family that can't understand why we haven't made an arrest yet."

"I understand that," DeBerry said. "But *they've* got to understand that we've got to have cold hard proof. Without it, we've wasted their time, our time, everybody's time. And worse—we've done Patricia no justice at all."

"David," Bryant said, "they want Church pulled from the case."

DeBerry stared at the lieutenant. "What?"

Bryant cleared his throat and began to speak, but the sheriff spoke first. "They want Jim pulled. They're not happy with the way the case is going."

DeBerry's shoulders dropped as he concealed a heavy sigh. "Jim Church is doing as good of a job as anyone else could do. He's a damn good detective. I don't give a shit who was working this case, we'd be no further along than we are right now." His voice was deeper and more firm than he intended, but he hoped he had gotten his point across.

"I know Jim's a good detective, David," Bryant said. "But he's getting frustrated."

"Christ, Grady, we're *all* getting frustrated." DeBerry sprang from the chair and walked to the window. The sun was beginning to fade into the horizon, leaving downtown Greensboro chilled and dark. Greensboro's few towering buildings overshadowed the streets, darkening them into opaque, parallel lines.

"David," Barnes said, his voice softening. "Grady's right. If Church is getting burned out, he's not doing anyone any good."

DeBerry turned around slowly and faced the sheriff. "I know you're right, but we just don't have many other options right now, Sheriff. What good would it do to pull Church off and reassign it to Mac or Herb when they're just as burned out with it as he is?" He slowly walked back to his seat but continued to stand, his shoulders weighted with responsibility, and loyalty. "Mac and Herb both have their own cases they're also working. I just don't see how reassigning this case would make a difference."

DeBerry had already pulled every district detective, those normally assigned to property crimes, that he could. They had assisted in interviews, running down leads, performing many of the mundane but necessary tasks. Although the opportunity lay before him like a picnic spread, DeBerry resisted the urge to confront the sheriff on the Major Crimes Unit's lack of manpower. With only the four of them—DeBerry, Church, McBride, and Byrd—serving a county half a million strong, it stood to reason someone was going to be slightly overworked. "What if," he said, the wheels beginning to turn, "instead of reassigning it, we ask for outside help?"

"You mean another agency?" Bryant asked.

DeBerry nodded. "What if we call in the SBI? Give Church a partner."

Barnes leaned back in his chair. "Anyone in mind?"

DeBerry sat down but leaned forward, a flicker of hope and excitement slowly working its way into his mind. "What about Harold Pendergrass? I know he's worked mostly vice, but I think he and Church would work well together."

Barnes slowly nodded. "Harold could handle a

homicide. I know he can. I worked with him several times when I was working vice."

Barnes and Bryant looked at one another. Bryant shrugged his shoulders. "Can't see that it would hurt anything. I think it's worth a shot."

"Go ahead and set it up," Barnes told DeBerry.

"Thank you, Sheriff." DeBerry quickly stood and started out of the office.

"David," the sheriff cautioned, "If we don't see some movement soon, though, we're going to have to look at it again."

DeBerry nodded. "I understand, Sheriff."

The sergeant wasted no time getting back to his own office, where he closed the door and put in a call to the State Bureau of Investigation.

At forty-nine, Special Agent Harold Pendergrass had been around law enforcement all his life. His father and his younger brother were with different police departments in North Carolina, another brother was with the Highway Patrol, and his older brother was in his fifth term as sheriff of Orange County also in North Carolina. To the Pendergrass family, law enforcement wasn't a career choice, it was a way of life.

Pendergrass was in his twenty-third year with the SBI and anxious to broaden his investigative wings. He liked working vice. He still caught a thrill by putting away low-life drug dealers. He still enjoyed his work. But he wanted a homicide. He wanted the challenge.

DeBerry hung up the phone, then called Church into his office.

"Starting tomorrow morning, Harold Pendergrass is going to be assisting you." He watched Church for a reaction—any reaction but saw only relief.

CHAPTER TWENTY-EIGHT

Summer 1996

Out of sheer frustration, Ronnie Kimble agreed to an interview with Church and Pendergrass. Church didn't care if Ronnie was getting frustrated, feeling badgered, or growing angry at the investigation. He couldn't have been any angrier or frustrated than Church.

Church had arranged for Ronnie to meet him and Pendergrass at the SBI office in Jacksonville, near Camp Lejeune. If the nervous tension Church had heard in Ronnie's voice when he arranged the meeting proved right, Church didn't want a break in the case to come at Camp Lejeune. If—and Church knew it was a big if—Ronnie broke, he'd rather it happen away from the base, where he and Pendergrass wouldn't be at the mercy of military jurisdiction.

Church and Pendergrass were restless as they waited in the parking lot for Ronnie. Summertime in Jacksonville, North Carolina, would try anyone's nerves, the humidity nearly unbearable. But it wasn't the heat or the sweat that dampened the back of Church's shirt that had him on edge. Church looked at his watch. Ronnie was already ten minutes late. "If he don't show," he mumbled.

"He'll show," Pendergrass said. "He knows it'll look *real* bad if he doesn't."

Pendergrass, dressed in a heavily starched, white button-down shirt, sharply creased khakis, and dark sunglasses, looked every bit the government agent.

Church looked at him and laughed. "How do you get those shirts so starched?"

"I ask the cleaners to double it."

"Don't they charge you extra for that?"

"Not if I smile real pretty." He lifted his shades and treated Church to a sample of his smile. Where Church was country-boy polite, Pendergrass was city-boy charm. His graying hair added to his suave character, making one wonder how he had been so successful in dealing with roughneck drug dealers. It was rumored, though, that he had to be trained how to dress the part. Grease-stained T-shirts and faded jeans weren't part of his wardrobe.

As Pendergrass lowered his sunglasses, Ronnie pulled into the parking lot.

"There's our boy," Church said, holding his breath for a moment.

They watched the pickup slow to a crawl, then park. Ronnie got out of the truck and slowly approached. He had an older model, full-sized cassette recorder tucked under one arm. He stopped within a few feet of the investigators.

"I told you to come alone," Ronnie said, staring hard at Pendergrass.

"Agent Pendergrass has been assigned to help me with the case. We're working as partners now."

Ronnie was quick to shake his head. "I don't like it. I told you I'd talk to you and only you. No one else."

Church lifted his hands trying to calm the Marine. "It's okay, Ronnie. Pendergrass and I are working as a team now. Anything you wanted to tell me, you can tell him. You ought to be happy about it, Ronnie. It shows we're dead serious about finding out who killed your brother's wife, right?"

Ronnie stared at the men with dagger-like eyes, then shook his head. He began pacing in small circles. "I don't like it. I told you to come alone."

"I can't do that anymore, Ronnie. Pendergrass and I are a team now. We count on each other, just like we're counting on you to help us find Patricia's killer. You want to help us with that, don't you Ronnie?"

Ronnie glanced nervously around the parking lot. He ran his hand over his hair. He gnawed on his bottom lip. Then, suddenly, he glared hard at Church. "Well, all right. Let's get this over with. I've got to get back to the base."

As they entered the office, Agent Walt House, an SBI polygraph expert, rose from behind a desk. "Looking sharp, Pendergrass," he said and laughed.

The men shook hands. Then Pendergrass introduced House to Church and Ronnie. "Agent House is going to be assisting us today, Ronnie."

Immediately, Ronnie tensed and backed toward the door. "I told you, Church, just you and me! And now you're trying to trick me into some lie detector test! This is bullshit."

Quickly, Church tried to smooth things over. "No one's trying to trick you into anything, Ronnie. We're just trying to get to the bottom of some things, that's all. Besides, a polygraph will work to your benefit providing you have nothing to hide, right?"

Ronnie paced around the room, glowering at the three men. "I don't like it, Church," he repeated again and again, his eyes narrowing each time.

There was a noticeable change in Ronnie Kimble, the young man Church had talked with in the past. There was now an edginess, a certain guard that wasn't present in the chatty, emotion-charged boy of last year. His emotions were still running high, but it wasn't grief he was expressing now. It was a cold, bitter anger.

"Ronnie, everything we're doing, we're doing for Patricia," Church said. He slowly approached, hands open and extended. "You want to help us, don't you? You want to help Patricia, don't you, Ronnie?"

Ronnie suddenly halted and pointed an angry finger at Agent House. "Either he goes or I go."

Church backed away. "Okay, no problem. We'll do it your way, Ronnie. No polygraph."

"You're damn straight it's my way. You don't have a choice." He arrogantly rocked back and forth on the balls of his feet. "And I say we're wasting time."

Church and Pendergrass looked at each other. Pendergrass then led the way into a small interview room. He closed the door behind them. Ronnie took a seat at the table.

Once they were all seated, Ronnie set the recorder on the table. He fiddled with the large buttons, pressing several before hitting the correct one. Then in a move that surprised both Church and Pendergrass, Ronnie tucked both his hands under his thighs and leaned slightly forward. "Let's do it," he said, staring directly at Church.

My God, Church thought—he's been coached. Someone's told this boy to watch his body movements.

Church eased into the questions as Pendergrass took notes. Frequently, Ronnie glanced over at Pendergrass and repeated an answer, ensuring the agent accurately recorded what was said.

But moments into the interview, Ronnie's belligerent attitude changed. His eyes welled with tears, his lips quivered.

"Is there something you want to tell me, Ronnie?" Church asked softly.

Ronnie bowed his head as tears fell onto his cheeks. Moments, an eternity of them, passed in silence. Each tense second brought Church's heart further into his throat.

"Tell me, Ronnie. Tell me what's on your mind."

"I want to tell you, but . . ."

"But what?" Church's heart thumped furiously; his mind raced. Stay focused, he thought. Stay with him. Church wanted to glance at Pendergrass to see if he, too, felt a breakthrough coming, but under no circumstances would he take his eyes off Ronnie. "Talk to me, Ronnie. Tell me what's on your mind."

Ronnie slowly shook his head. It was a move so small, it would have passed unnoticed had Church not been watching him so intensely. "I can't . . ." Ronnie said, his voice a shaky whisper.

"Ronnie—you're under an enormous burden right

now. Why don't you get it off your chest?" Although the urge to leap across the table and grab Ronnie by the shoulders was strong, Church mustered restraint.

Pendergrass had stopped writing. He watched as Ronnie's emotions swelled.

"Ronnie," Church spoke slowly, carefully, enunciating each word. "Did your brother kill his wife?"

Ronnie's shoulders heaved. His entire body shook. Suddenly, he took a deep breath and looked up, staring directly at Church. "No. I would tell you if my brother had killed his wife."

"Do you know who did?"

The seconds were as excruciating as their gazes were intense.

"Ronnie—talk to me. Do you know who killed your brother's wife?"

In one quick second, Ronnie squared his shoulders, swatted away the tears from his cheeks, and vaulted up from the chair. He jerked up the recorder, punched the off button, then stormed out of the office.

Church leapt from his chair and rushed after him. "Ronnie, wait!"

"It's over, Church."

Church and Pendergrass hurriedly followed him out into the parking lot.

"Ronnie, wait!" Church begged.

Ronnie threw up his hand and waved the detectives back. "I said it's over, Church."

"Come on back, Ronnie. Just you and me this time. One on one."

"No!" Ronnie wiped at his reddened face with the back of his hand. "You want to talk to me, talk to my lawyer." He jumped in the pickup, gunned the engine, and was gone before Church could reach him.

They stood and watched him as he swerved in and out of traffic, accelerating through a yellow light.

"Damn!" Church shouted, pounding the hood of his car.

CHAPTER TWENTY-NINE

The phone rang with a resonating blast. Eric Thompson rolled over and snatched it from its cradle. "Hello," he mumbled. He glanced at the alarm clock on his nightstand. It was a little after midnight.

"You ready?"

"Ted?" Eric pulled himself up and sat on the edge of the bed. "Ted, it's after midnight."

"Duh, like I don't know that. Meet us at the church on Highway 62."

Eric shook the sleepy fog from his brain. "Ted, what are we—"

The line went dead. Eric stared at the receiver for a moment before hanging it up. He then slipped out of bed and pulled on a pair of jeans and a sweatshirt. It was the middle of January 1997, and the cold would rip right through him. Besides, he didn't know if this would be one of Ted's quick trips or if they would be awhile. Either way, Eric wasn't prepared for the cold.

Eric Thompson had known Ted awhile. They were

roughly the same age, mid-twenties. At one time, they were best friends—friends enough that Eric had served as an usher at Ted and Patricia's wedding. He had come to know the couple through South Elm Street Baptist Church and had worked off and on for Ted at Lyles' Building Supplies.

Eric came from a good family, a hardworking, churchgoing family. His respectful upbringing showed in his calm, gentle demeanor. But this latest adventure of Ted's was playing on Eric's conscience and testing his loyalty. Denial was only good for so long.

"Everything okay?" Eric's father asked, poking his head into his son's bedroom.

"Yeah, it was Ted. He wants me to meet him."

"At this hour?"

Eric looked at his father and shrugged. He had as many questions as his father did. The difference was, Eric knew some of the answers. He just didn't want to admit them even to himself. But even more pressing than his discomfort with the whole situation was his fear.

Eric drove the short distance from his house to the Sure Foundation Baptist Church off Highway 62, near the 220 bypass. He dimmed the headlights as he pulled into the gravel parking lot. The beam of a flashlight beckoned him toward the back of the church.

There, he met up with Ted and Mike Melton, another employee of Lyles'.

"About time," Ted snapped.

"Sorry." Eric's gaze wandered over a stack of lumber loaded on the back of Ted's truck. Two solid oak doors, still encased in shrink-wrap, lay on top. "You sure these guys want to get rid of this stuff?" Eric asked, knowing in his heart the answer.

Ted laughed. "It's extra, Eric. I worked another deal."

Eric and Mike looked at one another. Their eyes met. Mike looked away.

"Are you two going to help, or are you just going to stand there?" Ted tossed a two-by-four onto the truck.

These late-night outings had been going on well over a month. With each one, Eric grew uneasier. Lumber, doors, windows, generators, even go-carts had found their way from building sites across the county to Lyles' Building Supplies. It didn't matter if it was a new home site or a church, Ted had "worked a deal" with the owners.

Eric grabbed a two-by-four and flung it up on the truck.

The following morning, although he wasn't scheduled to work, Eric dropped by Lyles'. He wanted to talk to Ted, or Mike, or anyone. Stealing from construction sites was bad enough, but stealing from a church . . .

The thefts were weighing heavily on Eric's mind and heart. It wasn't just the fear of getting caught that bothered him—it was the whole thing. Stealing was wrong. It went against everything he had been taught, everything he had been raised to believe. Still, the fear of getting caught wasn't nearly as great as Eric's fear of Ted.

Things had changed over the months. Ted had

changed. But today, fear or not, Eric had to talk to someone.

Mike Melton was outside on the lot, marking last night's haul of lumber. He squinted against the blaring sunlight as Eric approached.

"Ted around?" Eric asked. He lightly butted the toe of his sneaker against a stack of wood.

"He's inside, in the office."

Eric slowly nodded. He turned and started to walk away.

"Hey," Mike called quietly. He glanced around the lot before continuing. "You know anything about Ted's wife's murder?"

A searing knot grabbed Eric's stomach. He quickly looked toward the office, then stared at Mike. "Just what he's told me. You?"

Mike shook his head. "I looked up some old newspaper articles about it at the library, though. Kind of weird, don't you think?"

Eric looked down at the ground and kicked at the dirt. "Yeah," he said in a voice so low he wasn't sure Mike had heard him. Just as well, he thought. He wasn't sure he trusted Mike Melton.

Mike was a charmer, a modern-day con man, getting away with anything and everything he could. His movie-star good looks and brilliant smile saw him through most any situation. Mike was the same age as Ted and Eric, married with a young daughter. He was working his way through college and had come to work at Lyles' a few months earlier. He and Ted had struck up an easy friendship that crossed the boundaries of employer and employee.

Still, there was no honor among thieves, Eric

thought. But who else was he going to talk to? Although they had yet to speak of it, Eric sensed Mike was growing as uneasy as he was. He also sensed another common factor—a fear of Ted.

"I think one of us needs to talk to Ted," Eric said. The words escaped before his mind could hold them back.

Mike leaned against the stack of wood and slipped the marker into his pocket. "I was thinking the same thing. It's getting out of hand."

Eric continued looking at the ground, at the tiny puffs of dirt moving beneath his sneaker. "He's out of control. We're going to get caught."

"It's like he's daring the cops to catch us," Mike said, his voice ringing with uncharacteristic excitement.

"He's making fun of them. It's like he's flaunting it in their faces."

"You're talking about her murder, aren't you?"

Eric looked up. He gazed around the lot and wondered where everything had gone so terribly wrong. "Maybe. I don't know anymore. I just don't know *anything* anymore."

Their eyes met. They held their gaze for a moment.

"*You* want to be the one to tell him we want out?" Mike asked.

Finally, Eric turned and slowly walked away. He entered the building and was on his way to Ted's office when he heard footsteps approaching from behind.

"What are you going to say to him?" Mike whispered, walking briskly to catch up.

Eric stepped behind an aisle of wallboard. Mike glanced around, then followed.

"I don't know yet. I just know I'm not comfortable doing this anymore."

"Doing what?" Ted asked, seeming to appear from nowhere.

Eric's heart jumped. He stared blankly at Ted, then turned to Mike.

Ted laughed. The sound cut through the awkward silence like a jagged saw. "You guys," Ted said, shaking his head, a brutish smile twisting his lips. "Come on back to the office. I've got something I want to show you."

Ted waltzed away as quickly as he had appeared. Eric willed himself to breathe again and saw Mike do the same.

When they entered the office, Ted was sitting behind his desk with a stack of books laid out before him. "Look at these," he said, tossing the books to Eric.

Never Say Lie—How To Beat A Polygraph Test. The next, *Ultimate Sniper*. The next, *How to Build a Silencer.*

Eric stared at the books, then looked at the others. The titles were different, but Eric assumed the content was the same. Snipers. C-4 explosives. Beating interrogations.

Eric's blood turned cold. What in God's name had happened to the Ted he used to know? Or, had he ever *really* known Ted at all?

"Quite a collection," Mike said.

"Damn straight." Ted reared back in his chair. His

feet landed with a heavy thud as he propped them on his desk. "Pretty good reading, too."

"What do you need all this stuff for?" Eric asked, apprehensive of the answer.

Ted let out a belly-jarring laugh that faded into a sinister snicker. "Oh, you never know when you may need some of this information." He tossed a glass paperweight in the shape of a cross high into the air, then continued pitching it upward like a baseball. "Got another pickup tonight. I can count on you guys, right?"

Eric swallowed hard. "Ted . . . Mike and I have been thinking—"

"No, see, that's your first mistake." Ted dropped his feet and leaned forward. He turned the cross over and over in his hand, gently fingering its arms. "I don't pay you to think."

Mike stepped forward. "Ted, we're taking too many chances. The cops are getting close. You've said yourself they're watching you."

"I've also said they're a bunch of dumb-asses, *Mikey*."

"They're not as dumb as you think. I've heard through the grapevine they're starting to link some names. There's been too many thefts for it to go unnoticed."

Thefts. The word boomed in Eric's head. It was the first time one of them had actually spoken the word and suddenly, it seemed vile. Like taking the Lord's name in vain, it was a word foreign to Eric's vocabulary.

"Are you guys going to help me or not?" Ted stared at the cross, then tossed it onto a stack of invoices.

"I'm telling you, Ted, it's too risky."

"No, I'm telling you—*Michael*—I call the shots around here. I'll say when it's too risky."

"And what are you going to do if we don't want to help?" Mike asked, his voice a bit too shaky to project his normal confidence.

Ted, his eyes cold as steel, glanced from one to the other. "I'll kill you."

Mike guffawed. Eric's heart stuck in his throat as Mike's hearty laugh drizzled into a pitiful snivel.

"And don't think I can't get away with it." Ted lightly fingered the barrel of his new 300 Win-Mag. "I have for over a year now." He turned and stared at a framed portrait of Patricia hanging on the wall behind his desk. It was a wedding portrait—an exquisite display of a radiant bride.

CHAPTER THIRTY

Detective Herschel Wagner had been through so many different sheriff's administrations, he had lost count years ago. He had more experience than most of the sheriffs he had served under combined. Wagner was the proverbial bulldog, the thorn in a criminal's side. He hid his aggressive nature well under a low-key persona but took humble pride in never having lost a case.

He worked property crimes in the Sheriff's Department's third district, a wide area that took in Pleasant Garden and ran westward to the High Point city limits. Nothing made Wagner angrier than a thief's blatant arrogance. Stupidity, he could deal with. But arrogance just wouldn't be tolerated.

"Thirty-two thefts," he mumbled, the words coated in bitter disgust. He studied the latest report and sneered. Sure Foundation Baptist Church. "Lowlifes," he muttered, referring to thieves low enough to steal from a church.

He flipped through his notes from a few of the

previous burglaries and focused on a name one of the victims had given him. It had been just a hunch, the victim had told him, but there was something about the guy, something suspicious. He was too charming, too smooth. His name was Michael Melton. Wagner typed the name into the computer, and smiled. "My, my. What a coincidence." He printed the report and carried it into his sergeant's office.

"Remember the boy I was telling you about, the one I wanted to talk to about these burglaries—Michael Melton?"

"Yeah, what about him?" Detective Sergeant John Davis asked. He looked away from his computer screen and stared at Wagner.

"Guess where he works?"

"Where?"

"Lyles' Building Supplies."

Davis continued to stare at Wagner. He pushed away from his desk, his forehead creased with thought. "With Ted Kimble?"

Wagner nodded, his grin rapidly spreading.

"*Holy shit*. Does Major Crimes know this?"

Wagner shrugged. "I don't know. Why would they, though? I'm sure they know the names of everyone who works out at Lyles', but they wouldn't know anything about the burglaries, would they?"

Davis slowly shook his head. "I don't know. I doubt it. They leave the property crimes to us."

"Still want me to talk to Melton?"

Davis thought for a moment. A former homicide investigator himself, John Davis knew the ins and outs. He knew the rules. Homicides took precedence. It didn't matter how many burglaries, how many thefts, how many of anything his unit had, Davis knew the line of importance.

"Let me talk to DeBerry first," he said. "Let him know what's going on."

There were days Davis missed working homicides. He missed the moment of satisfaction he got from bringing justice to a victim's family. But he had no qualms or regrets when the district sergeant's position became available. He jumped at the new opportunity. Never one to look back, he was happy with the promotion and content with his new assignment. He'd be the best damn district sergeant they'd ever had.

He dialed DeBerry's number. The phone rang only once when Davis heard the familiar voice.

"DeBerry," he answered hurriedly, breathlessly bypassing normal telephone etiquette of reciting rank, name, and department.

Boy, they're busy, Davis thought. "Hey, Dee, got something you might be interested in."

"John Boy!" DeBerry exclaimed and laughed. "What you got?"

Davis filled DeBerry in.

Afterward, Davis stepped into Wagner's office. "Work him," he said and smiled.

The cold night air whipped through Eric Thompson's jacket. He shivered and pulled it tighter around himself. He replayed over and over the conversation with Mike and Ted. The cops were closing in.

It didn't matter. The threat of the police seemed only to make Ted more determined. Maybe it wouldn't be such a bad thing if we did get caught,

Eric thought. The prospect of going to jail couldn't be any more frightening than the prison he was currently living in.

"How do you like this baby?" Ted asked, a broad smile on his face. He patted the seat of a rented forklift as if it were a prized car. "Forget all that lifting shit. This thing will load it up a lot faster than we ever could." He climbed into the seat and cranked the motor.

"Ted, this is stupid!" Mike nearly shouted, glancing around the deserted parking lot of Home Depot. "I told you that detective came to see me today. Ted, they're getting close!" He jumped out of the way as the forklift lurched forward.

"You got your walkie-talkie?" Ted asked Mike.

Mike jammed his fingers through his hair and paced in circles.

"I said, have you got your walkie-talkie?"

"Yes, I've got the damn walkie-talkie!"

"Then get over on the other side of the store and keep a lookout. Go!"

Eric stared at the forklift and shook his head. He watched as the forked thongs slid under a stack of plywood.

"You got the scanner, right?" Ted asked him.

Eric slowly nodded.

"And you do have it set to the Sheriff's Department?"

Again, Eric nodded. Then he turned away.

CHAPTER THIRTY-ONE

January 1997

Mitch Wheeler watched his wife Debra fix Rebecca a bottle. Debra had their daughter propped on her hip, the little girl's legs around her mother's belly, heavy with another child.

"Can I do anything to help?" Mitch asked. Ronnie and Kimberly Kimble would be there any minute. The two couples had made dinner plans.

Debra glanced around the kitchen. "You can put away the dishes and make sure Joshua is cleaned up."

Four-year-old Joshua Wheeler ran up and down the stairs of the two-bedroom apartment, testing how many steps his little legs could skip before missing. Mitch shook his head, smiling, and wondered where his son got the energy.

Mitch had become friends with Ronnie Kimble while the two were stationed at Camp Lejeune. Although Mitch had been away from the Marine Corps for months, he and Ronnie had kept in touch. Mitch had moved his family to Lynchburg, Virginia, after leaving the Marines and was enrolled in the seminary at Liberty University.

Ronnie had called the day before and had told Mitch that he and Kimberly would be in the Lynchburg area. Ronnie was scheduled to undergo a series of sleep-disorder tests at the Naval Medical Center in Portsmouth, Virginia. When finished, Ronnie wanted Mitch to show him around the campus of Liberty University. Ronnie had been contemplating what to do with his life after the military and had decided, like his father, that he had received a call into the ministry. Although he still had a few months left with the Marine Corps, Ronnie was expecting to receive a medical discharge. With the sleep-disorder tests, he hoped the Naval Medical Center would confirm what he suspected but the Camp Lejeune doctors seemed unable to verify. Unable to stay awake, Ronnie was sure he was suffering from narcolepsy, but the doctors at Camp Lejeune weren't convinced. After their own battery of tests showed no obvious problem, at Ronnie's urging, they arranged for more sophisticated testing to be done at the medical center.

Mitch was concerned about Ronnie's sleep disorder but elated his friend had received a call into the ministry. He had met Ronnie and Kimberly for lunch and had shown them the campus between classes. They had been fortunate enough to meet the university's chancellor, Dr. Jerry Falwell, and Ronnie shared his concerns about his sleep disorder. He was afraid he wouldn't be able to stay awake through class.

"You don't mind if I ask Ronnie and Kimberly to stay with us, do you?" Mitch asked Debra.

Debra smiled. "No, not at all. I'm looking forward to meeting Kimberly."

Mitch knew Ronnie and Kimberly's money was tight. It was tight for everyone. He couldn't have in good conscience let them stay another night in a hotel. Besides, it would just be for a day or two. He finished putting away the dishes and wiped down the counter.

When the doorbell rang, Mitch went to the door smiling. After the hugs and introductions, Mitch carried Ronnie and Kimberly's bag upstairs to the kids' room and hurried back downstairs.

Ronnie was wrestling with Joshua, pretending to let the boy get the best of him and shouting fake screams of pain. Debra and Kimberly encouraged the act with their laughter.

"You all ready to go eat?" Mitch asked. "I don't know about you guys, but I'm hungry."

"Yeah, me too," Ronnie said. He stood and ruffled Joshua's hair, that same broad smile covering his face.

"Oh, before we go, do you mind if I use your phone?" Kimberly asked. "I want to call my mother and let her know where we're staying."

"Sure. It's right this way," Debra said and led Kimberly into the kitchen.

Kimberly was holding the phone to her ear, a puzzled expression on her face. She twisted the phone cord in her fingers, rolling it into spiraling knots. "What does he want this time?" she asked. She sighed heavily and closed her eyes. "I'll just call you when we get back."

She hung up the phone and frowned.

"What's wrong?" Ronnie asked.

"Nothing. Momma was on the other line and couldn't talk."

"Oh. Well, you can talk to her when we get back." Ronnie smiled and pulled on his coat.

"It was Detective Church. Again."

"What?" Ronnie asked, his voice rising to a childish squeal.

"She was talking to Detective Church. He called again." She looked concerned, but it was Ronnie's reaction that startled the Wheelers.

"What does he want with us?" Ronnie screamed. He slammed his fist against the counter, then suddenly fell to the floor. He lay there like a child, kicking his feet and pounding his fists against the tile. "Why won't he leave us alone?" he cried, over and over.

"Ronnie—it's okay," Kimberly pleaded. She tried to console her husband but was as perplexed as she was embarrassed.

Mitch and Debra looked at one another, both too shocked to say anything.

"Church is just doing his job," Kimberly said. "That's all." She helped Ronnie sit up and smoothed his hair.

"He's harassing us, that's what he's doing. He *will not* leave us alone."

Kimberly looked at Mitch and Debra. "I'm sorry. It's just that it's been a pretty stressful time."

It had been a year and three months since Patricia's murder. Although her name occasionally still came up in Mitch and Ronnie's conversations, the subject for the most part had faded over time. Right after it first happened, Ronnie had talked about it nonstop with Mitch. How could someone do this to Patricia, Ronnie had asked over and over again. Mitch had listened with a sympathetic ear and more often than not responded with the one thing he knew best—prayer. But now, Mitch wasn't sure how to respond. He couldn't remember seeing Ronnie so upset. Even right after Patricia's murder.

After a few awkward moments, Ronnie finally collected himself. "Let's go eat," he said, his voice flat and weak.

On the way back from the restaurant, Mitch adjusted the rearview mirror and caught Debra's reflection from the back of the van. She and Kimberly were chatting, occasionally laughing. Kimberly had been able to move past Church's phone call, but Ronnie couldn't dismiss it.

"What does he want from us?" Ronnie asked, his voice low, barely above a whisper. He sank further into the passenger seat and stared out the side window. "Why does he just keep on and on?"

Mitch wasn't sure Ronnie was directing the question to him, or if he even wanted an answer. But Mitch felt inclined to say something—anything—to cut the tension that had plagued them throughout dinner. "He's just doing his job, I suppose."

Ronnie sighed and continued staring out the window.

Mitch eased the van to a halt at a stoplight swaying above the intersection. "So what did Kimberly think of the university?" he asked, eager to change the subject.

"She liked it." Ronnie shifted his weight and

brought his gaze forward. "I don't know how she'll do, though, being this far away from her momma and daddy."

Mitch laughed. "Oh, she'll get used to it. It was hard on Debra at first, too, especially with the kids, but she adjusted." He glanced at Debra in the rearview mirror. Despite all the hardships, they had so much to be thankful for.

The light turned green. Mitch gently pushed the accelerator. He didn't like icy roads, but as he had done with his life, he put his trust in the Lord. "Kimberly will get used to being away from her family," he said, carefully navigating the van through the intersection. "Besides, if she's going to be a minister's wife, she had better get used to it. There's no telling what church you might be led to." He smiled at Ronnie, but it went unnoticed. Ronnie had turned back to the side window and gazed out. Mitch wondered what it was he saw.

"I may not even be able to enroll," Ronnie said quietly. "I guess it just depends on the test results."

"But Dr. Falwell didn't seem to think your sleep disorder would affect your studies," Mitch replied.

"Yeah, but he don't know how bad it is." Ronnie seemed to relax a little, allowing his shoulders to slump slightly forward. "No one seems to know how bad it is except me."

"Are you saying the doctors don't believe you?"

"They act like it sometimes. Like I'm just making it up, or something."

"But you've been tested before. And those tests showed a definite problem, right?"

"I suppose," Ronnie said, his voice falling back into a whisper.

In fact, the previous tests had shown no significant sleep disorder. Ronnie had been so unconcerned with the results, he failed to mention the negative outcome even to his wife.

Mitch waited patiently for Ronnie to continue. He always continued. He always went into lengthy explanations when a simple "yes" or "no" would suffice. But this time, he didn't.

After a moment of heavy silence, Mitch resorted to what he knew best. "Maybe we should pray about it."

Ronnie didn't respond.

"God has a way of lifting burdens, you know?" Mitch smiled, but again it went unnoticed. Of course he didn't really need to explain the power of prayer to Ronnie. He had been brought up in the church. His father was a minister. It was their way of life.

"Maybe I'm not cut out for the ministry."

The remark hit Mitch like a hard-thrown sucker punch. When had Ronnie changed his mind? He had been so excited to see the campus, even more excited after meeting Dr. Falwell. "Why would you say something like that?" Mitch asked as he turned the van into their parking lot. He pulled into the empty spot beside Ronnie and Kimberly's car.

"Maybe I'm just not cut out for it. I've done things, Mitch. Things in my past."

"Ronnie, we've all done—"

"Brr—it's cold!" Debra said. She and Kimberly hurried out of the van and up the sidewalk. Debra carried Rebecca close against her chest while Kimberly held Joshua's hand. Without the warmth of a running motor, the biting cold quickly penetrated the van.

Still in the driver's seat, Mitch pulled his coat tighter around himself to fight off a shiver. Ronnie seemed oblivious to the freezing temperature. "Ronnie, we've all done things in our past we're not proud of. I certainly have." The cold air chewed at his fingertips. He desperately wanted to take the conversation inside. "That's the beauty of being born again. We're washed clean of our pasts. We're forgiven."

Ronnie turned to Mitch. "You don't understand." His usually warm, bright eyes were as cold and piercing as the air that swirled around them. "I have a *haunted* past, Mitch."

Mitch had never seen Ronnie like this. His stare was so cold.

But like a child on a teeter-totter, Ronnie's mood suddenly swung high. "But we'll talk about that later. Right now, I'm freezing!" He laughed like a little boy, like Joshua would have, and bolted from the van into the warmth of the Wheelers' apartment.

CHAPTER THIRTY-TWO

Mitch tried to put the image of Ronnie's steel-cold eyes behind him but was finding it difficult. Once inside the apartment, he immersed himself in his Bible studies. He could always count on the Word for guidance.

He sat down at the small kitchen table, his Bible spread open before him. The pages were dog-eared, the leather binding worn smooth. He needed a new one, but Joshua needed a new coat, the van needed new tires, and the baby Debra carried would need . . .

Oh, well, he thought. The baby could make do with Rebecca's hand-me-downs. And he'd just have to make do with this old Bible. Besides, it was like an old friend. And one doesn't just toss away old friends.

Ronnie soon joined him at the table, his own Bible clutched in his hands.

"I don't really understand the Apocrypha," Ronnie said. His face was filled with such boyish wonder, such innocence, it was hard for Mitch to believe he was talking to the same man whose gaze only a short while ago had cut through Mitch's very soul.

"The Apocrypha or the Apocalypse?" Mitch asked.

"The Apocrypha—Father Soutiere and me talked about it a lot."

Mitch smiled. Soutiere, one of the base chaplains at Camp Lejeune, was a good man. "The Apocrypha is—" Mitch stopped. The noise of the children in the living room was increasing. Ronnie glanced over his shoulder into the living room, his brow furrowed with confusion.

Mitch was used to the chaos and had learned to adjust his concentration above it. But it was obvious Ronnie was having trouble.

"Why don't we go upstairs to study?" Mitch suggested. He hoped in the still of the quiet, Ronnie might turn whatever was troubling him over to the Lord.

Ronnie pressed the palm of his hand against his eyelid as if trying to press away a troubling thought. "Yeah, okay."

Ronnie followed Mitch up the stairs and into the Wheelers' bedroom. As Mitch sat on the edge of the bed, Ronnie closed the door behind them. "Now, what were you saying about the Apocrypha?"

"The Apocrypha," Mitch continued, "is basically several books of the Old Testament that were edited out of the final version of the King James. They have some historical significance but—"

"What do you mean—*edited out*?" Ronnie sat down beside Mitch on the edge of the bed. "Who edited them?"

Mitch thought about it for a moment. "Well, I don't

really know. They really have no prophetic importance, though."

"Yeah, but who gave someone the right to edit God's word?" Again, Ronnie pressed his hand against his eyes.

"I don't know, Ronnie. I've never questioned it."

Ronnie stood up and paced back and forth in front of the bed. "I don't understand what makes someone think they have the right to cut out part of God's word. It's not right, Mitch." He had picked up his pace, his feet falling heavier on the floor. "What gives someone that right?"

"It's like with any other book, Ronnie. Unimportant parts are going to be edited out."

Ronnie spun around and glared at Mitch. "But who are we to say what's important and what's not? Maybe there was one verse in those chapters that would have changed someone's life. Maybe they would have changed . . . my life." His voice fell into a whisper.

Ronnie sank beside Mitch onto the bed, then lay back, staring at the ceiling. "I just don't know anymore, Mitch."

"Don't know what?" Mitch softly asked.

Ronnie sighed heavily. "Just things."

"Maybe we should—"

"Yeah, I know—pray about it. That's the answer to everything, isn't it?"

For a moment, Mitch thought he detected an edge of sarcasm in Ronnie's voice. But he dismissed the thought, knowing Ronnie believed in the power of prayer as much as he did.

"Read from the Book of Psalms," Ronnie said, still

staring at the ceiling. "It's always been my favorite."

Mitch flipped pages and began reading the first verse his gaze fell upon. "O Lord my God, in thee do I put my trust; save me from all them that persecute me, and deliver me: Lest he tear my soul like a lion, rending it in pieces, while there is none to deliver.

"O Lord my God, if I have done this, if there be iniquity in my hands: If I have rewarded evil unto him that was at peace with me; (yea, I have delivered him that without cause is my enemy:) Let the enemy persecute my soul, and take it; yea, let him tread down my life upon the earth, and lay mine honour in the dust. O Lord—"

Ronnie sprang from the bed. He circled the room, fast, then faster, his jaw clenched. His breathing was coming in short, quick gasps. Suddenly, he slammed his hands against his head, squeezing his temples.

"Ronnie . . . you okay?" Mitch spoke slowly, quietly.

"No," he mumbled. "Nothing's okay. I did it, Mitch." He turned and faced Mitch, his cheeks wet from a steady stream of tears. "I killed her. I killed Patricia."

The world Mitch Wheeler knew stopped. This new, strange world began spinning and spinning like one of his son's toy tops.

"I shot her in the head, then set her body on fire."

Mitch willed his heart to beat again. He willed himself to breathe. "Why, Ronnie?" His voice was so soft, so shallow, he wasn't sure he had actually spoken the words.

"Because my brother paid me to do it." His face softened as he stared at Mitch. It was as if he were wrapped in the comfort of a soft, gentle blanket of peace. With the honesty of a child, he asked, "Can I give the money Ted paid me to the university? To further God's word?"

"No!" Mitch forced down the bile surging up into his throat. His chest tightened. He was overcome with revulsion. "It's blood money."

"Well, I don't want it." He sounded as if he were talking about a piece of discarded furniture that could be put to use elsewhere.

"Ronnie—you've got to turn yourself in!" Mitch immediately regretted the statement. He didn't want to further upset Ronnie.

Ronnie began moving around the room. He fingered a framed portrait of Mitch and Debra that was sitting on the dresser. "I'll never turn myself in," he said in a low voice. "I'll die first."

Mitch hesitated before speaking again, asking the Lord for guidance. "You've got to tell the truth, Ronnie. You have to tell the authorities."

Ronnie spun around and faced Mitch. He grinned a twisted, ugly grin. "I have told the truth. They've just never asked the right questions." He stared again at the portrait, then sat back down beside Mitch on the bed. "Do you go to Hell if you kill yourself?"

"I . . . I don't know." Mitch wanted to run, he wanted to grab his family and flee, but was terrified of what the murderer sitting beside him would do. Would he come after them? Was he carrying a gun? *Or would he choose the coward's way out like he was talking about?*

"I don't want to go to Hell," Ronnie said, his voice breaking as he began to cry again. "I've already asked the Lord for forgiveness. That's enough, isn't it?" He wiped his nose with the sleeve of his shirt. He took a deep breath, then sighed. "Besides, it was her time. And when your time's up, your time's up. Right?"

A tingling chill ran the length of Mitch's spine. "Maybe we should pray," he said, his voice cracking.

Ronnie wiped his face with the backs of his hands and nodded. He raised himself from the bed, turned around, and lowered himself to his knees. He looked at Mitch like Joshua had done every night—eyes wide, hands clasped together beneath his chin, head slightly bowed, ready to say prayers.

Mitch knelt at the edge of the bed and knelt beside Ronnie. He closed his eyes. "Our Lord, our God, forgive us of our sins . . ."

CHAPTER THIRTY-THREE

The Lord is my shepherd; I shall not want. He maketh me to lie down in green pastures: he leadeth me beside the still waters. He restoreth my soul: he leadeth me in the paths of righteousness for his name's sake. Yea, though I walk through the valley of the shadow of death, I will fear no evil.

Mitch recited the prayer that night over and over again. If he had ever needed the comfort and protection of the Lord, he needed it now.

He saw every shadow that passed in the hallway. Every ice-laden tree branch that fell against the roof, he heard.

Like a shepherd watching over his flock, Mitch thought as he gazed at Debra from the corner of the bedroom where he sat. She slept restlessly, often stirring, often reaching out for him. Joshua and Rebecca slept soundly on their mattress on the floor. No sleep for Mitch. He was too frightened to sleep.

Across the hallway, in his children's bedroom, slept Kimberly and Ronnie. A murderer. A cold-blooded murderer.

He wondered how he could have put his family in such danger. How could he have allowed this to happen? He had his suspicions about Ronnie when he was still stationed at Camp Lejeune, but they were just that—suspicions. Like rumors, they were best left unsaid.

But if Mitch had his suspicions, why then did he allow Ronnie to even visit? Because he wanted to believe. He wanted to believe Ronnie's story. He needed to believe it.

How many times had Ronnie denied his involvement? How many times had he openly wept for Patricia, for his own brother?

Did Kimberly know? Did she know she was sharing a bed with a killer? Certainly she knew. She had to. But she was so sweet, so open, so caring. Maybe she didn't know. Or maybe she, too, didn't want to believe it.

Debra stirred. She called out to Mitch softly. Mitch moved to her as quietly as he could, as quickly as he could. "Shh," he whispered.

"What are you doing still up?" she murmured.

"Just thinking. Go on back to sleep." He stroked her hair and softly kissed her forehead. "You need your rest."

She mumbled and snuggled down against the pillow. Soon, she was still again.

Mitch pressed his face into the softness of her hair

and couldn't stop himself from crying. His hand rolled softly over the blankets, searching for the curve of her belly, searching for the new life growing inside her. Searching for hope.

A tree limb snapped and scratched against the window. Mitch bolted upright. His heart thundered in his throat. His mind raced.

The steady *tick-tock* of the alarm clock was amplified in the silence. 5:00 A.M. Only a little while longer.

Ronnie had agreed he and Kimberly would leave early that morning. It was best, Mitch had thought, not to anger or upset him any more and agreed to let him stay the night. Besides, it would have alarmed Debra if Mitch had insisted the couple leave. The roads weren't too bad, but still, Debra would have questioned the abrupt change of plans.

Mitch quietly rolled from the bed and sat on the floor beside his children. He pulled the downy blanket over Rebecca and tucked it under her dimpled chin. Mitch fingered the golden curls that framed her perfect face.

Blessed be the pure in heart, for they shall see God.

How could such goodness, such innocence and purity, live hand-in-hand with such evil?

A rustling noise came from across the hallway. A shadow moved across the far wall. It was only when he saw two figures move in the shadows that he knew it was almost over. Ronnie and Kimberly were leaving.

His gaze never left the bedroom door as he carefully eased himself beside Debra onto the bed.

It was only when he heard the front door open and

close and the sound of a car engine being cranked that Mitch finally closed his eyes.

Debra stretched and yawned. The morning sun shone brightly through the window, cascading ribbons of light over the rocking chair in the corner of the bedroom.

She felt the soft fluttering within her expanding belly and reached to touch it. She smiled.

She yawned again and reached for her robe, gathering it around her as she headed downstairs. "Morning," she said as she entered the kitchen.

Mitch was at the stove aimlessly stirring eggs. He was wearing the same clothes he had worn the night before. "Mitch . . ."

Something was wrong. Debra knew her husband too well.

"Mitch, what's wrong?"

He wouldn't look at her. Instead he continued stirring the bowl of eggs.

"Mitch?"

Suddenly, an overwhelming thought slammed into Debra's mind. An ugly, horrible thought. She turned and glanced back up the stairway. The stairway she had just come down. The stairway that led to where she and her children and her husband had slept just hours before. "Where's Ronnie and Kimberly?" she asked, slowly turning back around to face her husband.

Mitch dropped the fork he had been using. He turned to Debra. His eyes were deep pockets of red.

"Mitch . . ."

Tears rushed from his eyes. He gasped for breath as he tried to speak.

Debra jerked her hand to her mouth to stifle her scream. "Oh God! He did it, didn't he? He killed Patricia!"

CHAPTER THIRTY-FOUR

"Still got that gun?" Mitch asked. He sat in the diner booth nervously shredding a napkin.

Joyce Wheeler looked at her little brother with disbelief. This wasn't Mitch. The nearly black circles shadowing his usually bright eyes, the forehead creased with worry . . . and now a request for a gun?

She slowly took a sip of coffee. "Mitch, what's wrong?"

He glanced around the tiny diner, then stared back down at the napkin. "I'm just worried about Debra and the kids. That's all."

"So you're going to start carrying a gun? Mitch, that's not like you."

Nothing made sense to her. It started with his panic-filled phone call that morning and insistence in seeing her right then. She had offered to come by the apartment later that evening. No, Mitch had nearly screamed into the phone, he had to see her right then.

"Does Debra know you're here?"

"Of course she knows."

"Then why couldn't I come by the apartment?"

Mitch took a deep breath. He ran his tongue over his dry, cracked lips. "We're going away for a couple of days. She's packing a few things."

"Dear God, Mitch—what have you gotten yourself into?"

Mitch glanced up at his sister with tears in his eyes. "I can't tell you right now. Just trust me. Please."

"You call me in a panic, you look like you haven't slept in ages, you ask me for a gun, and now you tell me you're going away for a few days. And I'm supposed to just hand you this gun without any questions? Mitch—"

"Joyce, please! I know it probably sounds insane. But I just can't tell you right now." He slumped down in the booth and ran his hands over his unbrushed hair. "Everything will be all right. I've just got to do some thinking."

Joyce stared at her brother. Mitch had a good head on his shoulders. He thought things through and seldom gave way to impulse. And unlike a lot of people she knew who turned to prayer only when all else had failed, she knew Mitch would have already hit his knees. If this was the answer he had received, she felt no need to question it further.

"It's in the car. We'll get it when we go out."

Mitch nodded.

Later that evening, Mitch hurried through the crowded parking lot of the university's gymnasium. Liberty U was playing a home game. The deafening cheers blasted through the walls, reverberating into the cold night air.

Mitch ignored the jostling crowd and moved toward the half-court box seats. He needed advice. The only man he felt he could trust with the knowledge that had been thrust upon him was Dr. Jerry Falwell himself.

He spotted Falwell among a small group of constituents. Sequestered from the boisterous students, Falwell was following the action on the court intensely.

Mitch's heart pounded as he pushed his way through the crowd. As he drew closer to Falwell, he could feel his adrenaline surging.

"Hey! You can't go there, son," a uniformed security officer called. He stepped in front of Mitch and blocked his way.

"I've got to see Dr. Falwell," Mitch said frantically.

"You'll need to call the office and make an appointment." The guard spoke in a loud voice, competing with the cheering crowd. "Dr. Falwell doesn't like to be interrupted when he's watching a game. Call the—"

Mitch didn't give the guard time to finish. He vaulted the railing and bolted toward the doctor.

"Hey!" the guard yelled.

As Mitch lunged for Falwell, another guard clamped his arm. Falwell turned and looked at the scene as more guards surrounded Mitch.

"Doctor Falwell—I've got to talk to you!" Mitch screamed. "Please, Doctor Falwell. Please!"

Falwell glared at the screaming young man for a moment, then waved the guards back. "Let him through. Let the boy through." He motioned Mitch forward.

The man in the seat next to Falwell moved back a row, allowing Mitch to sit next to the reverend.

"I'm Mitch Wheeler. I'm a student here at—"

"I know who you are, son. You brought a young friend of yours to meet me the other day. I believe he suffers from a sleep disorder?"

"Yes," Mitch said, choking on his words as he fought the urge to sob. "He's the reason I'm here. I don't know what to do, Doctor Falwell. I need guidance."

"What seems to be the problem?"

"Last night at my house, he confessed to a murder. He told me he killed his sister-in-law."

Church grabbed the phone on the first ring. "Detective Church, Criminal Investigations."

"Detective Church, this is Jerry Falwell, Jr. I'm an attorney at Liberty University."

Church raised his eyebrows. What in the world could this guy want?

"We have a young man here in our office with information you may be interested in."

CHAPTER THIRTY-FIVE

DeBerry leaned against one of the many bookcases in Attorney Jerry Falwell Jr.'s office and gazed out the window at the campus. The winter chill pressed against the glass. The campus was dead still, eerily quiet. Almost as quiet as the drive up to Lynchburg. DeBerry, Church, and Pendergrass had barely spoken, each cocooned in his own thoughts.

DeBerry imagined they were all thinking the same thing. Could this be it? Or would it prove to be just another dead-end? After almost a year and a half of grabbing a good lead only to run head first into yet another brick wall, they were just too damn tired to get excited anymore. Too tired to feel that rush of satisfaction.

The door opened. Falwell Jr. entered. Mitch and Debra Wheeler followed, clinging to each other, their faces kaleidoscopes of fear.

"Before we begin," Falwell said, "our client wants guaranteed protection for himself and his family."

DeBerry nodded. "If what he has to tell us warrants it, we'll arrange it."

Falwell looked at the sergeant. "It will."

The Wheelers sat down on a leather sofa. As Mitch recounted his story, DeBerry studied his eyes, his movements, and listened intently to the tone of his voice. It wasn't long before he felt the first tingling of that familiar rush.

"Ronnie told me he killed his sister-in-law," Mitch said in a soft, low voice. He gazed downward, squeezing his wife's hand. "He said he shot her in the head and then set her body on fire."

"How was Ronnie acting prior to this confession?" DeBerry asked. "What kind of mood was he in?"

"It's hard to say. One minute he was fine, the next he seemed angry. He kept going back and forth. That's what scared me so bad—I didn't know what to expect from him."

"Was he that way all night? Even at dinner?" Church asked.

Mitch nodded. "More or less, yes. But he had been fine earlier when I saw him at lunch and when he and Kimberly first got to the apartment. It was the phone call that seemed to set him off."

"You mean when I called Kimberly's mother?" Church asked.

"Yes. When her mother said she was talking to you, Ronnie just . . . he just lost it."

"What do you mean?"

"He fell to the floor—"

"Literally," Debra interjected. "I mean he *fell* to the floor. Kicking and screaming like a baby would have." She turned to her husband as if to apologize for having interrupted.

"It really took us by surprise," Mitch said. "We didn't know what to do."

"How long did that go on?"

"A few minutes, at least."

"What happened then?"

"He seemed to calm down a little, enough for us to go on to dinner, anyway. But he acted real strange the rest of the night. I mean, one minute he would be okay, the next he was real depressed. He talked about a *haunted past*." Mitch looked down. Again, he squeezed Debra's hand.

"Mitch," DeBerry asked, "did Ronnie say why he killed Patricia?"

With his head still bowed, Mitch answered, "He said his brother paid him to do it."

Church looked up at DeBerry.

Several hours later, after Mitch had told his story, DeBerry called Guilford County Assistant District Attorney Richard Panosh from Falwell's office. DeBerry filled him in.

"You've got your protection," DeBerry assured Mitch after he hung up. "We'll work out the details before we leave."

Mitch and Debra looked at one another, relieved, yet still troubled.

DeBerry sat on the edge of Falwell's desk in front of the young couple. "Mitch, would you be willing to talk to Ronnie again?"

Mitch's eyes widened. "I . . . I don't know," he stuttered, looking to Debra.

"What we'd like, Mitch, is for you to talk to him again—for him to repeat what he told you last night. You'll be wearing a recording device—"

"No." Mitch sternly shook his head as he interrupted DeBerry. "I'll talk to him, but I won't do that. That's nothing more than lying. And I'm not a liar."

DeBerry nodded. "Okay, then we'll work with what we've got."

DeBerry knew it would be hard for a jury to find doubt in Mitch's story. But a taped confession would have been nice.

Mike Melton walked back and forth along the secluded dirt road. He stuffed his hands into the pockets of his coat to warm them. A bitter cold front had swept the state, bringing heavy clouds that threatened ice.

Although it would have provided warmth, Mike was too nervous to wait in his car. He shivered against the cold and pulled his collar up around his neck.

Was he doing the right thing? He wasn't sure. Mike did know he was jammed up. He was afraid of Ted. He was afraid of the prospect of jail. But jail couldn't be any worse than the prison he felt he was already in. Telling a cop seemed the only way out.

A dark blue Taurus turned onto the dirt road and slowed. Mike swallowed the knot in his throat. Whether right or wrong, it was too late for him to turn back now.

The Taurus pulled alongside Mike. He opened the passenger side door and got in.

"What are you doing standing outside in the cold?" Sergeant Cameron Piner asked as Mike closed the door.

"It's not all that bad once you get used to it." Mike clasped his hands together and blew puffs of warm air into them.

"Yeah, and your hands aren't blue, either, are they?" Piner was young, good-looking, and had an easy manner about him. He had busted Mike a few years back for marijuana possession, and the two had formed a cautious alliance.

The low, hanging clouds began to spit an icy drizzle. Piner turned on the windshield wipers. He and Mike sat in silence for a moment listening to the blades scrape against the glass. "What's on your mind?" Piner finally asked.

Mike took a deep breath and let it out slowly. "I've messed up, Cam. I've messed up bad."

Back in Greensboro it was well after five o'clock when DeBerry, Church, and Pendergrass arrived back at their offices. They took the access elevator to the fourth floor of the Guilford County Courthouse and hurried into Panosh's office.

DeBerry had requested Panosh early on in the investigation. Panosh was one of the best homicide prosecutors in the county, if not the state.

He was a soft-spoken yet intimidatingly intense man who knew the law and took it seriously. In the courtroom, he was never one to grandstand or make a spectacular scene, choosing instead to use his knowledge of the law as his only weapon. Tall and thin with a runner's build, Panosh worked the courtroom with the cunning of a cougar. Narrowed eyes, jaw set. A smile was as alien to Panosh as the world was to a newborn.

"Close the door," Panosh said as DeBerry, Church, and Pendergrass entered. Not one for small talk, he went straight to the point. "Did he consent to wear a wire?"

DeBerry shook his head. "It's against his religion."

Knowing DeBerry and his off-the-wall nature, Panosh raised an eyebrow.

"I'm serious," DeBerry explained. "He feels it's a form of lying and is adamantly opposed."

"Did you express to him the importance of it?"

"Dick, he ain't going to wear one." DeBerry relaxed in the wooden chair and loosened his tie. "We're just going to have to go with what he told us."

"So basically what we've got is more hearsay."

Church's shoulders sank. He stood and strolled the room. "It's a confession, Dick."

"It's a third-party confession, and we're taking a chance going with it."

DeBerry sighed heavily and massaged his forehead. "Dick, I'm afraid this is as good as it's going to get. There is no smoking gun, there are no fingerprints. There are no eyewitnesses. This is it."

Panosh leaned back in his chair. He clasped his hands together and pressed his index fingers against his lips. Finally, he leaned forward, his arms on his desk. "Then we better make *damn* sure we've got every *T* crossed and every *I* dotted. There is *no* margin for error."

CHAPTER THIRTY-SIX

After the meeting with Panosh, DeBerry gathered his investigators. "I want every report double-checked, triple-checked, then checked again," he said as he closed the conference room door. "I want every witness interviewed again and their statements confirmed. If there's one loose end, I want it tied. And I want it tied *tight*."

"When do you think we can move?" Church asked.

"Not until every aspect of this case is thoroughly gone over and gone over again. I will not lose this one on a technicality."

"What about the thefts?" McBride asked.

"They're ready to issue warrants. One of the boys rolled over. They're not going to move, though, until we do." DeBerry lit a cigarette and hoped the sheriff would forget the building's no-smoking policy. "From this point on, everyone in this room should consider themselves gagged." He thumped a tail of ashes into a trash can, then paced back and forth in front of his men. "This case is not to be discussed with anyone outside this unit. No wives, no girlfriends, no fathers or mothers. I don't even want it discussed with patrol officers or the district detectives. I don't even want your goddamned dog to know about it. Is that understood?" He stopped pacing and faced his men. "Are there any questions?"

The men looked at each other and shook their heads.

"Then let's get at it. We've got a helluva lot of work to do."

March 31, 1997

Church bounded up the back steps. He hurried through the door and into DeBerry's office. Breathlessly, he tossed two manila envelopes on the sergeant's desk.

DeBerry turned the envelopes over in his hands and looked at the name on each one. Ronnie Lee Kimble Jr. was neatly typed on one, Theodore Mead Kimble on the other.

"Sealed warrants," Church said.

"Good. Call the troops." DeBerry stood and grabbed his coffee cup.

Members of the Crime Repression Team (CRT) soon joined the investigators in the crowded conference room.

As DeBerry fixed a fresh pot of coffee, Church pulled down a map of the county from the back wall and spread it on the table.

"For those of you who may be wondering what the hell is going on," DeBerry said, smiling at the members of the CRT, "if all goes according to plan, tomorrow morning you'll be assisting us in the arrest of Mr. Theodore Mead Kimble."

"Cool," one of the younger deputies said. There were smiles and high fives throughout the room.

"If you're not familiar with the area, familiarize yourself now," DeBerry said. "Study the map and memorize the street names. We'll use six cars. Two cars will follow Kimble as he leaves his home, two will then pick him up at Woody Mill Road, and then I want two on standby at Woody Mill and Highway 421."

"Does he always take the same route?" one of the CRT members asked. He leaned over one of the seated men to get a better look at the map.

"He has for the last year and a half," Church said. "Straight up Old Liberty Road to Woody Mill to the highway."

"He usually leaves the house around seven-thirty," DeBerry continued. "Which means we need to be in position no later than six forty-five. Sometimes he takes his mother to work, so there's a possibility she will be with him."

"What's the traffic like that time of morning?" one of the deputies asked.

"Heavy," Church answered. "But most of it will go on down to the next intersection."

"However," DeBerry cautioned, "we've got a middle school and a high school less than a quarter mile away from the Woody Mill intersection, so if Kimble's as little as ten minutes late, we run the risk of running into school traffic."

"Why not wait then and pick him up at work?" a deputy asked.

DeBerry quickly shook his head. "If he's going to run, we don't want it to happen in a populated area."

"You think he'll really try and run?"

DeBerry shrugged. "It's always a possibility. It's a precaution we have to take. We also have every reason to believe he *will* be armed."

DeBerry took a sip of coffee, then continued. "We've been told he carries a .22 with him at all times. You might say he never leaves home without it." The remark was met with a round of snickers that eased the tension. He sat on the edge of a computer stand and continued the briefing. "Now—while we're doing the fox-trot with Teddy Boy—Church, McBride, and Pendergrass will be in Camp Lejeune arranging for little brother Ronnie's discharge."

"We're nailing both of them?" a deputy asked.

"It's a two-for-one sale."

Sheriff Barnes shook his head and smiled. "The idea behind a simultaneous arrest is if they're both taken into custody at the same time, there's no chance for either of them to get a frantic phone call through."

"The sheriff's right," DeBerry said. "There *is* a purpose behind our madness." He looked over the small sea of faces, then asked, "Does anyone have any questions?"

"What's the chance Ted will try to run?" one of the younger deputies asked, a mixed look of eagerness and concern on his face.

DeBerry sighed. "Honestly, I wish we knew. But the truth is, we're dealing with Ted Kimble. There's no telling what he'll try to do."

It was after midnight when Church, Pendergrass, and McBride checked into the Jacksonville Days Inn.

Church and McBride shared a room, with Pendergrass next door.

Church sat on the edge of one of the beds and took off his shoes. He loosened his tie, stretched out, and closed his eyes. So many thoughts were running through his mind, he knew sleep would be long in coming. But it wasn't. Moments after he closed his eyes, Church was fast asleep. For the first time in a long while, he slept soundly through the night.

The alarm clock began buzzing at 4:45. DeBerry opened one eye and glared at the red glow of the clock, then pounded it into silence.

He pulled himself up to the side of the bed and snatched a cigarette from the nightstand. He sat with it dangling between his lips. "It's show time," he mumbled as he trudged off to the bathroom. He turned on the shower, then rambled into the kitchen for a much-needed cup of coffee. As he turned the kitchen light on, he stared at the calendar hanging beside the phone and burst out laughing. April 1, 1997. It was going to be some April Fool's Day for Ted Kimble. "Happy April Fool's Day, Ted. The joke's on you, buddy."

CHAPTER THIRTY-SEVEN

Since the night of the fire and Patricia's death, Ted had been living with his parents in their three-bedroom home in Julian. However, according to the insurance claim he filed, he was to rent his parents' home while they in turn moved into a single-wide mobile home located toward the back of the property. Neither Reverend Ron Kimble and his wife Edna, nor Ted for that matter, ever moved into the trailer.

For Ted Kimble, April 1, 1997 began like any other day. His mother poked her head into his bedroom around 7:00, telling him his breakfast was ready.

Ted rolled out of bed and pulled on a pair of faded jeans. He stretched, then padded into the kitchen in his bare feet, where a plate of freshly cooked bacon and eggs waited for him. He took a hearty gulp of milk from a glass his mother had poured for him and dove into the home-cooked breakfast.

"Busy day today?" Ron Kimble Sr. asked from across the table as he picked at his own breakfast.

Ted yawned. "So-so. Got to finish marking some inventory. Want to help?"

The reverend nodded in a noncommitting way. "I've got some business I need to finish up at the church first, then I'll be over."

Ted glanced at the clock on the kitchen wall. It was 7:15. He wolfed down the rest of his breakfast and hurried to finish getting dressed.

He dug a clean sweatshirt out of a stack of laundry his mother had done the night before, a flash of aggravation nipping at him. His mother knew which drawers his clothes went into. Why couldn't she take an extra five minutes and put them away?

After he dressed, he grabbed his wallet and watch from atop the dresser. He scooped up a handful of change, his hand nudging the urn that held Patricia's ashes. "Sorry," he mumbled. He stared at the urn, at the vase of fresh-cut red roses beside it. As he hurried out of the room, he anticipated a day not much unlike any other.

DeBerry drummed his fingers on the dashboard of the Taurus. He looked at his watch. He was strategically parked behind the Southeast Volunteer Fire Department, the car angled to give a clear view of both northbound and southbound Old Liberty Road. He looked at his watch again. Then a crackle came over the radio.

"This is car one—subject is pulling out of the driveway. Mama's with him."

DeBerry looked at his watch again. 7:35. They should be okay on time.

Another crackle. Another voice. "Car two—subject is in sight. I'm picking him up at Bedrock."

DeBerry glanced at his watch again. Moments later, another crackle. "Car three—I've got him at Dona Road."

DeBerry spoke into his radio. "Car three—what's the traffic like?"

"Clear. Only car on the road."

DeBerry breathed a sigh of relief. If everything had gone as planned, cars one and two should have circled around and should be approaching the Woody Mill intersection from the east. Car three should be bearing off any second to follow the same route.

"Car four—subject is in sight. I'm picking him up now."

DeBerry looked south. Ted's Jeep Cherokee crested the hill, followed at a distance by car four, a Crown Victoria. "Pull up on him, car four," DeBerry ordered. "Looks like he's picking up speed."

The Crown Victoria accelerated. "We're approaching Tabernacle Church."

"Take him." DeBerry threw his own Taurus into drive and pulled onto Old Liberty Road. "Just a little reminder, guys—he's armed."

Car four drew within a car length of the jeep Cherokee, then the deputy hit the lights. A siren warbled. The Crown Vic pushed to within inches of the Jeep's rear bumper, and the deputy motioned Ted over.

Ted turned onto Woody Mill Road, heading toward the highway.

"Come on, Ted," the driver of car four said to himself. "Don't be an idiot."

Slowly, the Jeep pulled to the shoulder of the two-lane road and crawled to a stop. As car four pulled up directly behind the Jeep, the other cars pulled behind it. DeBerry, though, pulled up past the line and angled the Taurus in front of Ted.

The deputy in car four took a long, slow breath, then got out of the car and approached the Jeep cautiously. Ted had already rolled down the driver's-side window and sat glaring at DeBerry.

"Are you Theodore Mead Kimble?" the deputy asked.

Ted feigned surprise, a nervous smile on his lips. "Yeah, I'm Ted Kimble. What's the problem?"

"Need you to step out of the car for a moment, Mr. Kimble."

"What's going on?" Edna Kimble demanded.

"It's okay," Ted said, turning to his mother. "I'm sure it's nothing."

"Need you to step out, sir," the deputy repeated. He kept a close eye on Ted's hands.

"Sure. No problem." Ted turned to his mother again. "It's okay. Everything will be all right."

Ted climbed down from the Jeep and glanced around at the caravan of unmarked cars. "What's the problem? Was I speeding?"

"No, sir. But you are under arrest. Do you have any weapons on you?" The deputy pulled a pair of stainless steel handcuffs from his belt.

"Under arrest? What the—"

"Do you have any weapons on you, Mr. Kimble?"

Ted jerked his head around to the Jeep. "Call my attorney!" he yelled at Edna. "Now!"

Edna frantically pushed the cell phone's buttons, her face flushed red.

The other officers had gotten out of their cars and approached the Jeep. DeBerry remained at the Taurus and leaned against the trunk. He thumped out a cigarette and casually lit it.

"Mr. Kimble, I asked you if you had any weapons."

Ted stuttered, seemingly confused. "There's one in the car. What are the charges? What am I being arrested for?"

"We'll talk about all that when we get downtown. Right now I need you to put your hands behind your back."

Ted pushed his arms backwards. The deputy clamped the handcuffs around his thick wrists. As he was being led to the Crown Victoria, Ted turned and peered over his shoulder. With a stare as cold and sharp as a dagger, he locked eyes with DeBerry.

At 8:00 A.M., Ronnie bounded into the chaplain's office of Camp Lejeune, ready for work. He had entered the office with a spring in his step, but the spring quickly turned into a thud.

"Ronnie Lee Kimble Jr.?" the military police officer asked. His partner beside him had an equally stoic expression.

Ronnie took a deep breath and held it a moment. "Yes," he answered in a slight voice.

"We need you to come with us back to our office, please."

Ronnie stared with wide, nervous eyes at the officer. "Wh . . . what for?"

"We have an order for your arrest, Mr. Kimble."

Ronnie fell pale as all color rushed from his expressionless face.

Later, in the office of the Judge Advocate General (J.A.G.), Ronnie sat across the table from Church. Pendergrass sat beside Church, and McBride sat next to Ronnie. The detectives waited patiently while officials prepared Ronnie's discharge papers. Although he was three weeks shy of completing his full term of service, due to the circumstances officials proceeded with his release.

As he had done in his earlier interview with Church and Pendergrass, Ronnie sat with his hands tucked tight under his thighs. "I ain't answering any questions," he said, his jaw jutting forward in mock defiance.

"I'm not asking any questions," Church said.

"Good." He nervously rocked back and forth on his hands. His gaze wandered around the room, focusing on anything but the detectives. "I want to call my lawyer."

"You can call when we get back to Greensboro."

"I have the right to a phone call." He glanced at Church but quickly looked away.

"Yes, you do. And you can make that call when we get back to Greensboro."

"This is bullshit."

Church shrugged. If he had learned anything through this year-and-a-half ordeal, it was that the Kimble brothers were unpredictable. They had cultivated a deep anger toward Church and DeBerry. Two hundred miles away from his home and family, Church wasn't about to let Ronnie make a phone call. Church would never want to alarm Brenda or his kids, but truthfully, he feared for their safety. Paranoid? He didn't think so. One should always take precautions when dealing with a time bomb.

"I've got to go to the bathroom," Ronnie said.

Church nodded. "Mac will go with you."

Ronnie glared at Church with spitting anger.

McBride escorted Ronnie down the hall and into the men's restroom. Once inside, the bravado fell away. Ronnie collapsed to the tiled floor and burst out crying, his whole body shaking with sobs. McBride stood in the corner and quietly watched the scene.

"Ronnie, if you want to talk, we'll listen," McBride said softly.

After a few moments, Ronnie pulled himself up to the sink and splashed cold water on his reddened face. He shook his head in jerky, spastic motions. "I ain't got nothing to say to you."

"If that's the way you want it. Haven't you got to go to the bathroom?"

Ronnie glared at him hard, then straightened his stance and walked toward the door.

McBride escorted him back to the office, and they retook their places at the table. Ronnie sniffled but squared his jaw.

"Ronnie, your brother was arrested this morning also," Church said.

"What?" Ronnie stared at Church. Then his glance shot around the room as if he were imagining the worst possibilities. "Ted was arrested, too?"

Church nodded. "Yep. Sure was. He's probably

talking to Sergeant DeBerry about now."

Ronnie stared at Church, then quickly looked away. "What was he charged with?"

"Same as you. *First-degree murder.*" Church relaxed and leaned back in the chair. He picked at a cuticle. "Did you know first-degree murder's a death penalty crime in this state? You ever worked a death penalty case, Pendergrass?"

"Oh, yeah. Quite a few," Pendergrass lied. "Usually when someone's looking at the death penalty, especially when there's someone else involved, one of them will start talking sooner or later. I guess when you're facing the death penalty, it's every man for himself."

Ronnie stared hard at Church, his eyes filled with fear.

Church sat up in his chair. He was satisfied they had planted the seed. Which brother would be the first to roll over on the other remained to be seen.

CHAPTER THIRTY-EIGHT

Sheriff Barnes stood in front of the floor-to-ceiling windows of his office and looked out at the news vans parked across the street. The reporters and their cameramen would be casually shuffling their way into the downstairs conference room anytime now, unaware of the subject of the press conference he had called.

After Church had called and told him Ronnie was in custody, Barnes sent notice to the local media. He kept the reason for the press conference to himself. Before going public, he felt it was only right that Patricia's family be told of the arrests in private.

There was always a touch of regret anytime an officer had to tell a family about an arrest. But the regret was often mixed with the satisfaction of having taken the first step toward acquiring justice for the victim and the family. Now, Barnes searched his heart for that spark of satisfaction, but it was slow in coming.

Telling the Blakleys that their former son-in-law had been arrested for their daughter's murder wasn't going to be easy.

Although the Blakleys had been pressing Barnes for months as to why Ted hadn't yet been arrested, Barnes knew they were still filled with doubt. As hard as it was for them to accept Patricia's death, it was even harder to accept that Ted, someone they had loved as their own, was responsible.

There was a soft knock on the office door. His secretary poked her head in. "The Blakley family is here, Sheriff."

Barnes sighed deeply and hesitated before responding. "Send them in." He walked slowly to his desk and waited.

Moments later, Patricia's mother and father, Richard and Sheila, and her brother Reuben and his wife Kristy, entered the office. They appeared nervous, a little confused.

"Morning, folks," Barnes said. He then greeted each one individually. He motioned them to a group of chairs in front of his desk and then perched himself on the edge. Slipping his hands into his pockets, he struggled to find the right words. "Folks, this isn't going to be easy. So I'm just going to come right out and say it." He took a deep breath before continuing. "We made an arrest this morning."

Sheila grabbed Reuben's hand.

"It's a good news/bad news type of thing," Barnes said.

Before the sheriff could continue, Richard broke in. "It's Ted, isn't it?" His lips were quivering as he spoke.

Barnes looked at each one of them, one at a time. "Yes. He was taken into custody at 7:30 this morning."

Sheila began to cry quietly. Barnes gave them a moment before he continued.

"Folks—you should know, too, that we also arrested Ronnie."

"Ronnie?" Reuben said, his voice filled with questions. "He was in on it, too?"

"From what it looks like, yes, we believe he was."

Sheila gasped and sobbed loudly. Richard slumped down in the chair. The large man looked somehow small, almost helpless as he, too, began to weep.

Breaking all the "don't become involved" rules, Barnes reached out and placed his hand on Richard's shoulder. When it came to this particular case, he doubted there was anyone in his entire department who hadn't broken that rule.

It was after five o'clock when Church, Pendergrass, and McBride arrived back in Greensboro with Ronnie, who was dressed in his military fatigues. As Church turned onto Sycamore Street, the street running beside the Sheriff's Department, his heart dropped to his feet. News vans from every television and radio station within a hundred miles lined the surrounding streets, boxing in the Sheriff's Department. Their mobile satellite receivers stretched upward. Reporters—television, radio, and print—swarmed the area.

"Holy cow," Church said. The sheriff had warned them about heavy media coverage, but Church wasn't expecting this.

"We better go through the tunnel," McBride said from the backseat. "At least we can close that off."

As Church slowly passed the front entrance of the

building, he noticed a large crowd gathered at the top of the ramp. They huddled together, their arms around one another for support. Church recognized some of them as members of Monnett Road Baptist Church.

"There's Mrs. Wilson," Ronnie said, staring wide-eyed at the scene. "And Mrs. Crutchfield."

"You better wave hello now," Church said, " 'cause we're going in the back door. Call Sarge and let him know we're here." He tossed his cell phone over the seat to McBride and circled around the block, carefully maneuvering around the reporters scampering about in the street.

After circling, Church drove into the underground tunnel and pulled as close as possible to the back access door where DeBerry and members of the Crime Repression Team waited. He had just parked when a crowd of reporters and cameramen rushed the tunnel. The CRT officers corralled the media away from the car and pressed them back.

Shielding his eyes from the camera lights, McBride got out of the car first and opened Ronnie's door. Church got out of the car and walked around to the passenger side. Together, he and McBride rushed Ronnie toward the door DeBerry held open.

Once inside, they walked into the magistrate's office. DeBerry had already secured the area. The magistrate sat waiting.

Outside the magistrate's small office, McBride leaned against the cold concrete wall. "Guess someone tipped off the media."

DeBerry smiled. "Sheriff called a press conference. It's been a fucking zoo around here."

"How'd it go with Ted?" Church asked.

"Like clockwork. Except his daddy's raising hell about seeing him. He's claiming pastor privileges and thinks he ought to be able to see him anytime."

"But he's not Ted's pastor."

DeBerry lifted his eyebrows and grinned. "Exactly."

Later that night, armed with search warrants, Sergeant John Davis used a hacksaw to cut through the locks on two tractor-trailers parked across the street from Lyles' Building Supplies. Davis shook his head as floodlights illuminated the contents of the trailers. Doors, windows, plywood, lumber, even a garden tub.

"That's about forty grand worth of building materials," he said, hopping down from the back of one of the trailers. He joined DeBerry, Church, a horde of other officers, and members of the Crime Lab.

Both Davis and DeBerry leaned against the back of DeBerry's car. "Better go ahead and start inventorying all this stuff," DeBerry told the sergeant of the Crime Lab.

"Want to go take a look in the office?" Davis asked.

DeBerry slowly massaged his forehead. He looked at his watch. It was pushing midnight. "Yeah, I guess. Ain't like I've got anything else to do tonight." Completely exhausted, he, Davis, and Church headed toward Ted's office. "I really do need to get a life," DeBerry said. Davis couldn't help but laugh.

Inside, Davis skimmed through Ted's survivalist library. *"Ultimate Sniper?"* he said, and showed the book to DeBerry. He continued skimming through the stack, reading the titles aloud. "What in the world does someone need with all this stuff?"

"Same reason they need this," DeBerry said. He shook his head as he turned a silencer over in his hand.

"Hey, DeBerry, look at this," Church said. He lifted the 300 Winchester Magnum.

"Well, I'll be damned. It ain't fair. Kimble got his gun, but I haven't got my yacht yet."

"Yeah, and you probably won't, either," Davis said, "not as long as you're in this line of work."

DeBerry sat down in Ted's chair and gazed around the cluttered office. Davis was right. None of them would ever get rich in this line of work.

Was it worth it? Was it worth the twenty-hour days, days when your mind and body longed for the numbness you knew would come when you passed the point of aching from the tiredness? Was it worth all the missed holidays and the busted marriages? Was it worth it, knowing that no matter how many criminals you arrested, the robberies wouldn't stop, the rapes would continue, and sometime, somewhere, someone else would be murdered?

His gaze moved slowly over the room, finally settling on Patricia's wedding portrait. He sat there awhile just staring at it, thinking back to Ted's arrogance the day he and Church talked to him at Lyles', the sour expression on his face when told he was under arrest.

He focused on Patricia's smile. Yeah—it was worth it. It was worth every minute.

CHAPTER THIRTY-NINE

The day after Ted and Ronnie's arrest, Eric Thompson and Mike Melton were arrested for their participation in the burglaries. However, unlike the Kimble brothers, both Eric and Mike were offered bail. Later that day, Church met with Detective Sergeant John Davis, Assistant District Attorney Dick Panosh, and Eric at Eric's attorney's office.

"Did Ted ever say anything to you about Patricia's death?" Church asked.

Eric half-shrugged. "Not that I remember." He nervously strolled around the office, too agitated to sit.

Standing in a corner of the office, Davis leaned against the wall and studied Eric. His nonchalant attitude wasn't working; Davis read right through it. The boy was nervous and scared.

"Ted never said anything at all?" Church pressed.

Eric pushed his fingers through his hair, then shook his head. "No," he said, his voice taking on a whining tone.

"Weren't you good friends with Ted?"

"Yeah, but we didn't talk about it too much."

"So you did talk about it. Just not very often, right?"

Eric squirmed. "He might have said a few things, but it was just in general conversation. Nothing specific."

"These few things that he said, do you recall what any of them were?"

Eric shook his head, gazing downward.

"You don't recall anything he said?"

"Nothing sticks out in my mind."

"You don't remember anything he said about his wife's murder? Come on, Eric, it wasn't like you were discussing the weather. Generally, discussions about a friend's murder stick out in someone's head."

"He said . . ." Eric stopped. Again he shook his head. "He never really said *anything*. We just didn't talk about it that much."

"You were an usher at their wedding, weren't you, Eric?"

He looked at Church, then quickly looked away. "Yes."

"Then you knew Patricia, too, correct?"

He nodded.

"Did you like her?"

Again, he glanced at Church. "Yeah—I mean, who didn't like Patricia?"

"I don't know, Eric. You tell me."

He looked away from Church and pressed his back against the wall. "He didn't tell me anything," he mumbled.

Davis was growing tired of the cat-and-mouse games. Particularly since he knew Eric wasn't coming clean. Davis didn't doubt he was telling the truth. But he was only telling a small part of it.

All of a sudden, Davis sprang toward the boy, blocking him from moving away from the wall. Davis pushed his face to within inches from the trembling boy's and shouted, "You think you're in trouble now, Eric? You ain't seen trouble if we find out you're lying to us!"

Eric's entire body shook. Davis was so close to getting the truth he smelled the boy's fear.

"I . . . I don't know anything," Eric stuttered and began to cry.

Davis slammed both his hands hard against the wall, the blasting *pop* coming inches from Eric's ears. "Look, you little punk, you're only facing felony larceny charges right now. You want to add accessory to murder to it?"

"No! I didn't have anything to do with it. I swear!" He was crying hard now.

Eric's attorney stepped between Davis and his client. "Eric, tell them what they want to know. Just tell them the truth, and it'll make it a lot easier on everyone."

Davis took a step back. "Felony larceny isn't anything to laugh about, but you stand a good chance of walking away from it, kid, if you'll work with us. The more you help us, the more you'll help yourself."

Eric's attorney turned to Panosh. "What exactly is he looking at, sentence wise?"

Panosh shook his head. "I'm not offering any deals. But Sergeant Davis is right. The more he helps us, the more we'll help him."

"You don't understand," Eric sobbed.

"Don't understand what?" Davis asked.

Eric buried his face in hands and, crying, slid down the wall.

"We don't understand what, Eric?"

"He said he'd kill me."

"Who said they'd kill you?"

Eric gazed up at Davis, then looked across the room at Church and Panosh. "Ted. He said he'd already gotten away with one murder."

"Patricia's?"

Eric slowly nodded.

"Did he tell you he killed Patricia?" Church asked.

"He said *he* didn't do it—but that his brother did."

Church looked at Panosh and Davis. Panosh motioned Davis back. There wasn't any need to press Eric harder. The boy was telling the truth. Fear was a common thread among those who knew Ted Kimble. Like an umbilical cord, it was the tie that bound them together.

CHAPTER FORTY

On April 9, 1997, nine days after their arrests, Ted and Ronnie Kimble were indicted by a Guilford County grand jury. Ronnie was charged with first-degree arson, conspiracy to commit murder, and first-degree murder. Ted was charged with conspiracy to commit arson, conspiracy to commit murder, first-degree murder, breaking and entering, felony larceny, and possessing a weapon of mass destruction—the silencer.

Both were denied bond. Because Guilford County was one of the only counties in the state with two detention centers, Ronnie was held in the Greensboro jail while Ted was transferred to the High Point facility.

In July, a judge earmarked both cases as capital cases, giving prosecutors the go-ahead to seek the death penalty. Reverend and Mrs. Ron Kimble stood not only to lose one of their sons—they stood to lose both.

The trial dates would be at least a year away. The brothers would be tried separately.

When it came to the Kimble brothers, though, detectives with the Guilford County Sheriff's Department had come to expect the unexpected.

November 1997

Sheriff Barnes hated to interrupt anyone's Thanksgiving but this couldn't be helped, nor could it wait. He called DeBerry and Church to his office, where they met with the jail supervisor.

"You're not going to believe this," Barnes said, shaking his head. "Our case against Ronnie could be in jeopardy. One of the female jailers has gotten, um . . . well—rather friendly with Ronnie Kimble."

"Oh shit," DeBerry said, the word dragging on into a disgusted whine.

Church closed his eyes for a moment and massaged his forehead. The sheriff was right. Church didn't believe it. At least he was having a hard time believing it.

"According to one of the other jailers, it appears a little oral sex may have taken place," Barnes said.

"Great. Just fucking great." DeBerry, in jeans and a sweatshirt, stood up and paced the room. "My Thanksgiving dinner's interrupted while Ronnie's getting blow jobs."

Barnes couldn't help a slight grin, but then returned quickly to the seriousness of the situation. "Our biggest concern is how much, if any, information has been leaked. Not so much what he's told her, but what she's told him."

"Christ," Church said. He, too, stood and strolled around the office, shaking his head at the unthinkable possibilities.

"She couldn't have told him much," DeBerry said. "She couldn't *know* that much. My men are still gagged, and Dick's got the DA's office gagged. If she's told him anything, it's rumor."

"You think she's a go-between for him and Ted?" Church asked.

The jail supervisor shook his head. "It's doubtful. She'd have no business being at the High Point jail."

"Apparently, this other jailer has also seen some letters that have been exchanged between Ronnie and the girl," Barnes said. "Internal affairs will launch a formal investigation tomorrow morning, but I want Ronnie's cell searched today. I want to know what's in those letters."

"Do I get you hard, baby?" DeBerry read from one of the confiscated letters. He, Church, McBride, Byrd, and Pendergrass were gathered around the table in the conference room sorting through the stack of letters. The letters, along with several suggestive photographs of the jailer in question, were taken from Ronnie's cell. He had them hidden in his Bible and complained loudly when his Bible was also taken as evidence. "Are you hard now just thinking about me? Are you thinking about my lips, my breasts . . ." DeBerry busted out laughing. "Jesus," he finally mustered.

They continued reading through each letter. Occasionally, a faint snicker or even deep-bellied laughs interrupted the silence.

"Well, I've seen a lot of reference to breasts and mouths and penises and buttocks, but nothing about his case," Church said, thankfully.

Pendergrass laughed at the sound of the various words coming from Church's mouth—each word slowly drawn out with precise enunciation, spoken with a syrup-thick Southern accent.

"What's going to happen to the jailer?" McBride asked.

"She'll be dismissed," DeBerry said. "Then the DA's office may bring charges against her. And Ronnie, for that matter. Sex with a custodial." He arched his eyebrows, reminding himself and the others of the seriousness of the matter.

Two weeks after the discovery of Ronnie and the jailer's affair, Ted stepped into the spotlight. On December 8, 1997, he pleaded guilty to the burglary and larceny charges and also to the charge of possessing a weapon of mass destruction—the silencer that was found in his office.

The courtroom was packed with Kimble supporters, all members of Monnett Road Baptist Church, as Ted tearfully begged the court's forgiveness and for mercy.

"Your Honor," Ted's attorney said, "my client was convinced by a former employee that stealing from construction sites would be simple. Mr. Kimble found it was easy and almost enticing, but now wants to set the record straight. He wanted to plead guilty so he could be truthful and accurate about what occurred."

"What occurred was, Mr. Kimble was the ringleader in an organized theft ring," Dick Panosh countered.

Reverend Ron Kimble and Edna sat on the first row behind their son with their heads bent and hands clasped tightly together. Edna quietly wiped away a tear as Ted was sentenced to four to five years on the theft charges.

CHAPTER FORTY-ONE

August 1998

Sixteen months after their arrests, two months shy of the three-year anniversary of Patricia's death, pretrial hearings and jury selection began in Ronnie Kimble's murder trial. The DA's office had chosen to try Ronnie first, knowing if they should for some reason lose a conviction with Ted, they'd never be able to get one with Ronnie.

During the pretrial hearing, Ronnie's attorneys fought hard to block the testimony of Mitch Wheeler, citing it broke minister confidentiality. But Panosh countered that Wheeler wasn't an ordained minister at the time of the alleged confession; he was a seminary student. DeBerry and Church breathed a deep sigh of relief when the judge ruled in their favor.

Jury selection took nearly a week. Several potenti[illegible] jurors were dismissed because of their oppositio[illegible] the death penalty. Finally, after questioning 1[illegible] tential jurors, 12 were seated and 2 were c[illegible] alternates.

On August 10, 1998, opening testimony began.

Each day, supporters of both families, the Blakleys and Kimbles, packed the courtroom. The numbers were for the most part equally divided. Most of the Kimble supporters were members of Monnett Road Baptist Church. Those supporting the Blakleys, including Eric Thompson, wore small purple ribbons pinned to their blouses and shirts in memory of Patricia. Like two warring factions, supporters of each family glowered at the other side, looking upon each other as the enemy. The Blakleys—Richard, Sheila, Reuben and Kristy—maintained their quiet, reserved demeanor.

From his seat beside Panosh at the prosecution table, Church kept a careful eye on the jury. One or two jurors looked at Ronnie with sympathetic eyes. That concerned him. He wished they could see the real Ronnie, the one who smiled and laughed and joked with his supporters each time he was escorted into the courtroom. Instead, with Ronnie already seated each time the jury was brought into the courtroom, they only saw the former Marine, a polite boy, solemn, with his head thoughtfully bowed in prayer. The double display turned Church's stomach.

Church was called to the witness stand during the [illegible]ond week of the trial and underwent a grueling [illegible] cross-examination. By the eighth hour, [illegible] growing weary but continued giving it [illegible] getting the best of Ronnie's attorney, [illegible]ow his own words to be twisted or dis-[illegible]

[illegible]he second week, with the jury out and [illegible]ked, Ted was brought in by the prosecution to testify. Wearing a prison jumpsuit, his hands and feet shackled, he took the stand and exercised his right to the Fifth Amendment.

It would be the last time Ron and Edna Kimble would see their sons in the same room at the same time.

Ronnie's defense was slipping. Although his attorneys were doing their best, Panosh was using circumstantial evidence and breath-stopping testimony to carefully construct an undeniable case of guilt.

Under extreme security, Mitch Wheeler retold how Ronnie had confessed to him his part in Patricia's murder. Debra Wheeler sat in the front row with the Blakleys and cried quietly while Mitch testified, his voice low and deep yet reverberating loudly through the dead-silent courtroom.

The jurors appeared to become uncomfortable during Mitch's testimony. Some squirmed in their seats. Several glared at Ronnie with questioning eyes. Ronnie sat with his head hung low, as did his attorneys. Defeat weighed heavily on their minds.

Ron Kimble, like his son, sat with his head bowed, his arm tightly around Edna's shoulder. Edna stared straight ahead, her face void of expression.

Following Mitch's testimony, shock waves ran through the entire courthouse as Dr. Jerry Falwell himself took the witness stand. Falwell had been subpoenaed by the prosecution to back up Mitch's testimony. Twelve bailiffs, members of the Crime Repression Team, and plainclothes deputies were added as a security measure.

Sheriff Barnes escorted Falwell into the courtroom and stood at the back door as the reverend recounted how Mitch Wheeler had told him about Ronnie's confession.

"The boy was terrified," Falwell said of Mitch. "It got my attention. And there's not much that can draw my attention away from a Liberty U basketball game." Falwell smiled his trademark, jovial smile, and it was met with grins throughout the courtroom. It was perhaps the only time smiles filled the courtroom.

After the testimony of Mitch and Falwell, two men ordained to the truth, the league of Kimble supporters quietly began to dwindle. How could they deny the testimony of two men who represented the righteousness of everything they believed in? The denial they had zealously clung to for so long was giving way to reality. For some, when they now looked at the Blakley family, their eyes were no longer filled with resentment and bitterness. Those feelings had now turned to sorrow and shame.

CHAPTER FORTY-TWO

Church tapped his foot anxiously. After six weeks of testimony, Judge Preston Cornelius charged the jury. Church studied each of the jurors carefully, paying particular attention to a young man in the back row. He was also concerned with an older black woman. They both showed obvious signs of sympathy toward Ronnie.

At 2:00, the jury began deliberations. Church, DeBerry, and Pendergrass stepped out into the hallway.

"We've got a problem with number three," Church said, referring to the woman juror.

Pendergrass nodded. He had been watching her, too. "If she's feeling sorry for him, there's no way we'll get a death sentence."

DeBerry leaned against the brick wall of the hallway. "I'll settle for a conviction."

Church looked at the clock in the hallway. It had only been fifteen minutes. The longest fifteen minutes he could remember.

At 4:30, they paced up and down the hallway, none of them moving too far away from the courtroom.

"This isn't good, is it?" Church asked DeBerry.

The sergeant shrugged. "Hard to say. You never know what a jury will do."

At 4:30, Judge Cornelius recessed court until 9:00 the next morning. Church's heart was heavy as he left the courtroom. It showed in his weary face.

"Don't worry about it," DeBerry said, hoping his own uncertainty didn't reflect in his voice. "It probably don't mean anything. It could still go either way. Go home and get some sleep."

Church nodded, knowing full well sleep would elude him that night.

At 10:45 the next morning, the detectives were growing more worried. The jury had already been out going on two hours, not to mention the three hours they were out the previous day. While DeBerry and Pendergrass resumed their pacing, Church slid down the wall of the hallway into a crouching position and ran his hands over his hair. He counted the speckles in the marbled floor. Like watching a silent movie, he replayed the last three years and wondered if there was something he should have done differently. He agonized over this interview and that interview. Was there someone he should have interviewed a third time? A fourth time? Was there one more question he should have asked? Maybe if he had pressed Ronnie just a little harder the day he and Pendergrass interviewed him. Ronnie had wanted to open up. He was carrying a deep, bothersome burden and wanted to unload it. Perhaps if Church had pressed just a little harder.

"Detective Church," Sheila Blakley said in a tiny, shallow voice racked with emotion. "I don't mean to interrupt."

"No, you're not interrupting anything," Church said as he stood up.

"I just wanted to say—regardless of what their decision is, I just want to say thank you for all you've done."

Church brought himself to look her in the eyes, to look into the eyes that for three years had haunted his every thought. The lines around her eyes were now more prominent, her cheeks more shallow, her auburn hair now streaked gray. Church softly smiled as he thought of the gray that now dominated his own hair.

"I was just doing my job, Sheila," he said tenderly. "We all were."

Suddenly, Reuben poked his head out the courtroom door. "Jury's back."

Both Sheila and Church took a deep breath. Church wrapped his arm around her shoulder and gave her a slight hug. "It's going to be okay," he said.

As the courtroom quickly filled to capacity, Church took his seat beside Panosh.

"Before the verdict is read," Judge Cornelius cautioned, "You may take this as a warning—I will not tolerate any emotional outbursts in this courtroom. If you do not feel you can control your emotions, please leave the courtroom now."

Church's heart was pounding so hard in his chest he feared Cornelius himself could hear it. He locked his fingers together to try to still them.

"We the jury," the clerk recited, "find the defendant, Ronnie Lee Kimble Jr., guilty of first-degree arson, guilty of conspiracy to commit murder, and guilty of first-degree murder."

"Sentencing will begin at 2:00," Cornelius said.

Church looked toward heaven and finally breathed.

Ronnie frantically tugged on his attorney's sleeve. "What happened? Why?" he demanded, his face contorted in disbelief. "How?"

"It's okay, everything's going to be okay," the man said, trying desperately to calm Ronnie.

Ronnie turned to his parents, to Kimberly, as the bailiffs cuffed his hands. "I love you," he said. But no words came. His emotions allowed only for him to mouth the words.

Kimberly collapsed into her mother's arms, weeping loudly. Reverend Ron Kimble bowed his head. Edna sat motionless, staring straight ahead at her son's vacated seat.

After years of bitter words and harsh feelings, Richard and Sheila Blakley embraced, each crying quietly on the other's shoulder.

Church offered his hand to Panosh and gave him a pat on the back. "Good job," he said.

In a complete turn of character, Panosh smiled.

Outside, in the courthouse parking lot, as the Blakleys were heading toward their cars, a loud, shrieking scream drew their attention. They turned toward the noise and to their horror, Edna Kimble was hysterically addressing them. "Murderers!" she screamed, "You're a bunch of murderers! You did this!"

Reverend Ron Kimble and a handful of steadfast Kimble supporters tried desperately to control her, holding her arms to keep her from lunging toward the Blakleys.

"She's calling *us* murderers?" Reuben said. He protectively pulled Sheila toward the car, unsure of what Edna would do. "Get in the car, Mama. Just ignore her."

Sheila stared at the screaming woman, confused and fearful. Finally, she slid into the backseat of the car, where she sat silently. In a perverted way, she understood Edna's fear. Losing a child was something Sheila wouldn't wish on her worst enemy.

"They're already assuming he's going to be sentenced to death," Kristy said after Reuben started the engine. "And they're supposed to be people of faith."

Reuben quickly pulled away from the parking lot, anxious to spare his mother any more of the stressing scene.

"An eye for an eye, a tooth for a tooth," Reuben said.

"Don't talk like that," Sheila said in a soft voice from the backseat. "That's not for us to decide."

Reuben glanced at his mother in the rearview mirror. There had been times throughout this whole ordeal when his own Christian values had been put to the test. His faith in everything he had grown to believe in had been tested. He had doubted, he had wondered why, and he had questioned God.

Now, he toyed with the true meaning of justice. Could he only be satisfied if Ronnie *was* convicted to die? Would it ease the pain or the loss?

Nothing would ever bring Patricia back. Reuben knew that. He knew the best thing for him, for all of them, to do was to let the court decide the punishment and to get on with their lives. To live each day being the best people they could be. Only by setting a true

Christian example could they bring true honor and justice to Patricia.

Besides, he heard Patricia say from somewhere in the far corners of his mind, one day both Ronnie and Ted would receive the only real judgment that matters.

"We can pick our friends," Ronnie's attorney said while addressing the jury before sentencing, "but we can't pick our family."

He slowly walked back and forth in front of the jury box, occasionally pointing to his weeping client, occasionally looking down in a quiet, contemplative manner. Throughout Ronnie's trial, both of his attorneys fought diligently to ban testimony or reference to Ted, often reminding the judge that Ronnie was on trial, not his brother. Now defeated, they built their quest for mercy on Ted's dominance over his younger brother. They painted a picture of two victims: one, a young bride; the other, an easily influenced, mentally impaired younger brother who only wanted to please.

But Panosh painted a different picture.

"Does Ronnie know right from wrong?" he asked Ronnie's father when the reverend took the stand as a character witness.

The reverend was slow to answer.

Panosh repeated the question. "*Does* Ronnie know right from wrong?"

"Yes," the reverend quietly answered, his head bowed low.

"No more questions, Your Honor."

It took the jury a little over an hour to return with

a sentence of life in prison without the possibility of parole. The young male juror whom Church had watched earlier turned his face away from the courtroom and wept.

The Kimble supporters were silent. The only sounds that could be heard were their quiet cries.

Before he was led away, Ronnie, dazed, looked back at his parents. "I love you," he said quietly.

For the first time in open court, Edna spoke. She stood, twisting a gnarled tissue. "Your Honor, may I please hug him before you take him?" she begged.

"No," Cornelius said firmly, "He's in the custody of the North Carolina Department of Corrections now."

"We never got to hug Patricia good-bye," Richard Blakley mumbled.

CHAPTER FORTY-THREE

November 1998

DeBerry hung up the phone, shaking his head. He couldn't believe what he had just been told. He stared dumbfounded into space, trying to make some sense of the information. He had seen a lot in his career, he had heard a lot. But this . . .

He got up from his desk and slowly walked into his detectives' office. He leaned against McBride's desk, slowly shaking his head, still unbelieving.

"What's the matter, Sarge?" Church asked.

DeBerry thought about it for a moment, carefully considering how to respond. "We've been summoned to Salisbury."

"Salisbury?" Byrd questioned. "What's in Salisbury?"

"The Southern Correctional Institute. And Ted Kimble."

Following Ted's plea to the burglaries, he was immediately transferred to Salisbury, about an hour's drive from Greensboro, to begin serving his four-to-five-year sentence. His trial date for Patricia's murder was set for January 1999.

"His trial's still a few months away," Church said. "What's going on?"

"Don't tell me he's ready to plead," Byrd said.

"No," DeBerry said, shaking his head. "He's not pleading—he's fleeing. The son of a bitch is trying to escape."

DeBerry, Church, and Pendergrass waited in an interview room at the Southern Correctional Institute. It wasn't Ted they were waiting for. They were instead waiting for an inmate named Larry Patterson. Hopefully, Ted didn't even know the three detectives were there.

An armed prison guard escorted Patterson into the room and closed and secured the door behind them. He positioned himself at the door, a constant reminder to Patterson as to where he was.

Patterson was tall, thin, and muscular. His hair was knotted and twisted into crude dreadlocks. DeBerry couldn't decide if he was Jamaican or if he just wanted to be. When Patterson finally spoke, DeBerry decided on the latter. His accent was as deep Southern as DeBerry's own, but at times Patterson tried unsuccessfully to add a more exotic twist.

"He's got detailed floor plans," Patterson said. "Got plans of this prison, the Guilford County Courthouse, and the jail."

"How do you know about these plans?" DeBerry asked.

"He showed them to me, man."

"Why you? You his bud?"

Patterson laughed. "Naw man, I ain't his bud. That son of a bitch is crazy, man. A crazy motherfucker."

"So how'd you hook up with him?"

"I'm supposed to be released next month, see. And he says he's got this job for me—on the outside. He showed me the plans and asked if I'd be interested."

"You were supposed to help him escape?"

Patterson shook his head, sending the dreadlocks into bouncing knots. "Naw, said he already had somebody on the outside to help him with that. He wanted me to do a special job."

DeBerry sat down across from Patterson at the table and stared him in the eyes. "What kind of special job?"

Patterson stared at the sergeant without flinching. "The motherfucker's got a hit list. He offered me a hundred grand to knock off some people."

DeBerry never took his eyes off Patterson, but could see Church turn away.

"Jesus Christ," Church said. "The guy never quits."

"Tell me about this list," DeBerry said to Patterson.

"It's mostly witnesses. Maybe a few cops." He glanced at Church, then DeBerry. "People scheduled to testify against him."

"And he was going to pay you a hundred thousand dollars to carry out these hits?"

Patterson nodded. "Told you the dude was crazy."

"What did you tell him?"

"Told him I wasn't interested. Told him I'd already pulled my time and was clean."

"What did he say to that?"

Patterson shrugged. "Said it was okay, no problem.

Said he had someone on the outside that would help, anyway."

Church stared at the names on the hit list. Gary and Rose Lyles: the former owner of Lyles' Building Supplies and his wife. The man who thought of Ted as a son, and the woman to whom Patricia had tearfully confessed her fear. Linda Cheek and her husband: Patricia's best friend and confidante. Eric Thompson and Mike Melton: two former friends of Ted's who implicated him in the burglaries. And Mitch Wheeler: a man Ted had never met but for whom he held deep disgust.

Beside each name on the list was the manner in which they were to have died. Electrocution, a robbery gone bad, rape, strangulation. The list went on, but Church stopped reading. A surge of bile turned his stomach and forced its way into his throat.

The list had been confiscated on December 21, when the SBI obtained a search warrant and searched Ted's cell. Also found, just as Patterson had said, were detailed floor plans of the Salisbury prison, the Guilford County Courthouse, and detention center.

The day before Christmas Eve, District Attorney Jim Kimel and Sheriff Barnes called a joint press conference.

"We want to warn the public," Kimel said to the room full of reporters, "that anyone involved in the Kimble case may be in danger."

"Have the witnesses on the hit list been notified?" one reporter asked.

"Yes," Barnes answered as he stepped forward.

"We've been in contact with each one and assured them my department will do everything within its power to see to their safety."

DeBerry, Church, and Panosh stood in the back of the room and remained quiet, allowing their respective bosses to field the fast-thrown questions.

"When were these murders to have taken place?" a television reporter asked.

"Over the upcoming holidays," Kimel answered. "According to the escape plans, Kimble had planned to escape tomorrow, Christmas Eve."

"Folks," Barnes said, "Let me emphasize, these were *very* detailed plans. These weren't just some fly-by-night sketches. We have no reason to doubt Kimble planned to carry this through."

"That's right," Kimel added. "That's the reason we felt the need for this press conference. We've learned through a source that Kimble implied he had help on the outside. We want anyone who may have been contacted by Kimble to know his plans have been discovered and precautions have been taken."

"Will these new developments have any bearing on Kimble's trial here?"

"No," Kimel said. "These new developments will be handled by the district attorney in that county. We are, however, in contact with them and are asking that they bring formal charges as soon as possible."

"What charges would that be?"

"Eight counts of solicitation to commit murder."

CHAPTER FORTY-FOUR

Ted's attorneys, his third set, scrambled to repair the damage. "This is absolutely ridiculous," said lead attorney Howard Zenner. He slammed the large case file on his desk. "They didn't call that press conference to *warn* the public, they called it to prejudice a jury."

Zenner's co-counsel nervously tapped his fingers on the desk. "A change of venue's our only hope for a fair trial."

Zenner rubbed his forehead, hoping to massage away a pressing headache. "Yeah, but where to? There isn't a county within a hundred-mile radius that hasn't heard *something* about this case." He stared out the office window at the urban landscape and considered their options.

Although Ted's trial was scheduled to start toward the end of January, soon after the December press conference, Zenner filed a motion for a change of venue. He felt there were just no other options.

Only a handful of people, including the Blakleys,

attended the hearing. Besides, it was just supposed to be a motion for a change of venue.

However, five minutes before the 2:00 hearing was to have started, Ted shocked everyone—including his own attorneys—and admitted his guilt in Patricia's death. He also entered an Alford plea, in which he would be treated as guilty without admitting guilt, in the eight charges of solicitation to commit murder.

"You enter this plea of your own free will?" the judge asked.

"Yes," Ted responded. Shackled and handcuffed, Ted showed little emotion. Or remorse.

By having pleaded guilty, Ted had saved himself from the possibility of receiving the death penalty. He stood to spend many, many years in prison, but death by lethal injection was no longer a fear.

Sheila Blakley, sitting beside Reuben in the front row, was at first too shocked to cry. Richard bit his bottom lip to keep it from trembling as he struggled to retain his composure.

Reverend Ron Kimble and Edna chatted quietly to themselves.

"Very well, then," the judge said after thoughtfully considering the plea. "Your sentencing hearing will be scheduled within the next six weeks."

All of a sudden, Sheila reached for Panosh and tugged on the sleeve of his coat. "The ashes—can we get Patricia's ashes back?"

Panosh bolted from his chair. "Your Honor, in light of the defendant's admission of guilt, the Blakley family would like to request that Mr. Kimble be ordered to return Patricia's ashes to them."

"Can you do that, Mr. Kimble?" the judge asked.

Ted bowed his head and slowly nodded. "Yes. They'll be returned." It was the first display of humbleness Ted had shown.

It was the last week of February, a week away from Ted's sentencing hearing. Judge Peter McKane sat in his chambers following a long day and opened the letter postmarked from a prison. He read through the letter once, then reread it again carefully. "I don't believe it," he mumbled to himself, shaking his head in disbelief.

He picked up the phone and dialed Dick Panosh's number.

"I just got a letter from Ted Kimble," he told Panosh. "He's wanting to reverse his plea."

March 1998

Sheriff Barnes stood outside the Guilford County Sheriff's Department and looked across the street at the courthouse. He looked upward, toward the roof, scanning left to right. His gaze moved down the right side of the building, across Market Street, and back up to the roof of the old courthouse. To the average eye, well-positioned snipers would have been impossible to see.

"What about the plaza level on the other side?" he asked as Lt. Bryant joined him. "Are we covered there?"

"They're already in place."

"And the bailiffs? How many have we pulled?"

"Four in the courtroom, two outside the doors doing pat-downs, plus eight CRT members stationed at each entrance and exit." Bryant tossed his cigarette as he and the sheriff made their way across the street. "He won't get far if he tries to run—that's for damn sure."

On the fourth floor of the courthouse, bailiffs had set up a makeshift check station outside the courtroom. Each person entering the courtroom was checked with a wand and patted down. Once the hearing started, the courtroom was locked and secured.

Each bench was filled to capacity, except this time, the majority of spectators were there in support of the Blakley family. After Ted's confession in January, the Kimble support had dwindled as church members began to accept the truth. The few that now lined the benches were those who had been asked by Ted to serve as character witnesses. Even Gary and Rose Lyles had been asked to testify on what a good person Ted was, and how Gary had grown to think of Ted as a son. Knowing full well that Ted had marked them for death, they politely declined the request.

At 11:00, Ted was led into the courtroom by armed guards. Shackled at the ankles, his hands cuffed and linked to a belly chain, Ted smiled at his mother and father.

Before they began, Judge Peter McKane recapped the letter he had received from Ted. "It's my understanding that you now want to reverse your plea of guilty? You claim you were coerced by your attorneys to enter this plea?"

Ted nodded in a spastic motion and stood. "Yes, Your Honor. If I may, I'd like to speak for myself in this matter."

Ted's attorneys turned to one another, a look of

total shock dominating their no-nonsense faces. Zeller quickly reached for Ted's arm. "Ted—don't," he begged.

Ted jerked his arm away. "No, it's time I tell the truth. May I speak on my own behalf, Your Honor?"

McKane looked at Ted's attorneys. "Mr. Zeller?"

Zeller threw his hands up. "This is all his doing, your honor. We knew nothing about it."

McKane sighed heavily. "Go ahead, Mr. Kimble. Speak your peace."

Ted struggled against the leg shackles and took a tiny step forward. "When I made that confession, I was under a great deal of stress. My attorneys had been pressuring me from day one to accept a plea bargain. They even tried to get me to put the blame on my own brother, saying it would make it easier on myself. But at the time, I couldn't bring myself to accept any kind of plea bargain because I knew I didn't do it. I knew I was innocent."

"But you stood in the courtroom down the hall and said that you *did* do it. Which is it Mr. Kimble?"

"I felt very intimidated, Your Honor. Not only by my own attorneys, but from all the law enforcement, too. They were all crowded around me. Every one of them had a gun, and they kept saying things like 'You're going to fry, Kimble,' 'Better give it up, Kimble.' Some of them had their guns drawn, and they were very angry and demanding. I was very afraid, Your Honor. I feared for my life. I wasn't in my right mind when I signed that agreement."

McKane stared long and hard at Ted then sighed heavily. "Court will recess while I consider Mr. Kimble's request. I'll be in my chambers."

It took him less than fifteen minutes to return to the courtroom.

"Mr. Kimble, let me ask you this. If you were so afraid, so intimidated, why did you wait over a month to request this reversal? Why didn't you do it as soon as you were returned to prison?"

Ted opened his mouth to speak, but no words came out. He stared down at the handcuffs binding his hands to his waist.

"Very well," McKane said. "Your request is denied, Mr. Kimble. Your sentencing will begin at 2:00."

A few minutes after two, Ted took the witness stand on his own behalf. As he fielded Panosh's questions, his put-upon, I'm-the-victim attitude brought on loud gasps and occasional snickers from the courtroom.

"My God," Church whispered to Panosh, "he actually believes himself."

Before Panosh closed, he glanced over his shoulder at the Blakley family, then turned back to the witness stand. "Mr. Kimble, back in January, you were asked by this court to return Patricia's ashes to the Blakley family. Are you prepared to do that?"

Ted swivelled the chair back and forth, his earlier humble attitude waning, giving way to his characteristic arrogance. "I don't have them," he said, smugly, turning toward the Blakleys. "I scattered them over Black Mountain before my arrest."

Sheila laid her head on Reuben's shoulder and quietly wept.

DeBerry and Church waited on the crosswalk for the traffic to ease. They were headed back from the courthouse to their office across the street. It had been a long four years. But today, maybe, *just maybe*, all the sleepless nights, all the frustrations, all the effort, had been justified. They knew nothing would ever bring Patricia back, but they hoped the Blakleys would find some small amount of comfort in knowing neither Ted nor Ronnie would ever walk the earth again as free men.

Church removed two cigars from the breast pocket of his coat. He handed one to DeBerry, then lit them both. As he took his first long, slow drag, he looked toward Heaven. "Rest in peace, Patricia. Rest in peace."

They looked at one another and smiled. It was a sad smile. But a smile just the same.

CHAPTER FORTY-FIVE

April 1999

Church busied himself putting old files back in order and rearranging the bookshelf behind his desk. A proud new grandpa, he placed the framed portrait of Dana and baby Amanda on the top shelf. In a couple of months, she'd be walking. In a few years she'd be starting school.

It had been over two years since Ronnie and Ted's arrest, going on four years since Patricia's death. Life goes on, Church thought as he gazed at the picture of his granddaughter. For every life that ends, a new one begins.

The phone rang, causing him to jump. "Detective Church, Criminal Investigations," he said into the receiver.

Suddenly, the blood rushed from his face. He felt both cold and hot at the same time. His breath seemed caught somewhere between his lungs and his throat.

"Are you sure it was him?" he asked, trying to keep his composure. "One hundred percent sure?" He twisted the phone cord into knots around his hand. "Which funeral home is he at?"

Church slammed the phone down, grabbed his coat, and tore out of the office.

Within a matter of minutes, he pulled into the parking lot of Hanes-Lineberry Funeral Home and bolted up the stairs. He flashed his badge at the director. "I need to see Ted Kimble."

"Ah—sure," the director stammered. "Right this way."

He led Church down a steep spiral staircase and into a back room. "We haven't begun yet to prepare the body, but as you can see—"

"Don't."

"Pardon?"

"I said *don't*. Don't prepare it yet." Church stood over the lifeless body, staring it up and down. "I want to run a test before you do anything."

"What type of test?" The director appeared uncomfortable at the strange request.

"I want him fingerprinted."

The body *looked* like Ted Kimble—the heavyset jowls, the short curly hair. Still, Church wanted to make certain.

The prison administrator on the phone had assured Church that it was definitely Ted Kimble who had been shot trying to escape. In this case, though, one man's word just wasn't enough.

Church called the Crime Lab and asked a favor of one of the technicians. "I know this is going to really sound strange, but I need you to fingerprint someone."

Church waited until the lab tech arrived and showed her the body.

"You want just the thumbs?" she asked.

"No. I want all ten rolled," he said, referring to all ten of Ted's fingers.

The tech looked at Church as if he were crazy. For a moment Church wondered if perhaps he was.

The following morning, Church called the lab before he had even taken off his coat.

"Jim—relax," the tech said. "It was Kimble. Through and through. It's over, Jim. It's all over."

Church eased himself into his chair and sighed. Perhaps it *was* finally over.

Later that week, the lab tech poked her head into Church's office. "You busy?" she asked in a small voice.

"Not too bad. What's up?"

She walked in and sat in the chair in front of his desk. She hesitated a moment, gnawing on her lip as if she really didn't want to say what was on her mind.

"What is it?" Church asked, his concern rising.

"You know those prints I did for you? I wasn't real comfortable with the results, so I sent them to the FBI lab. They came back this morning."

Church stared at her. His field of focus narrowed. Everything in the small, crowded room disappeared.

"Jim—they came back negative. That wasn't Ted Kimble."

Church bolted upright in bed, gasping for breath. Ice-cold sweat chilled his body and ran from his forehead into his eyes. Brenda stirred beside him, then sat up.

"Jim, what's the matter?"

"Nothing," he lied, quickly turning away from her. He swung his legs over the side of the bed. "Go back to sleep."

"Jim, this is the third time this week you've woken up like this."

"It's okay. It's nothing." He stood up and walked to the window. He gazed outside into the darkness, looking from tree to tree, from shadow to shadow. He then glanced at the Baretta on the nightstand.

He remembered the night he first met Ted Kimble, the night of the fire. The night at South Elm Street Baptist Church. He remembered Ted's cold, green eyes, the emotionless tone of his voice. He remembered wondering later that evening what he would have done had he been in Ted's place. If Brenda's, or Dana's, body had been found.

No, it wasn't Ted Kimble who haunted him. It was the greed-filled, cold-hearted, calculated way an innocent person had died. A living, breathing angel through no fault of her own fell into the depths of Hell. Patricia Blakley died a senseless, cruel death. *That* would haunt him forever.

EPILOGUE

On March 5, 1999, Ted Kimble was sentenced to 107 years in prison. He stands very little chance for parole. He must serve the time ordered for charges of both murder and arson. After his sentencing, he was transferred to North Carolina's Central Prison, a maximum-security facility located in Raleigh, North Carolina. He spends a good deal of his time isolated from the prison's general population for his own protection and so that prison officials can better monitor any escape attempts. Several young women whom he dated after Patricia's death visit him on a regular basis, still swayed by his charm.

On September 3, 1998, Ronnie Kimble Jr. was sentenced to life in prison without parole. For his own safety, he was transferred from one prison to another across North Carolina because of his inability to "adjust" to prison life. Now settled in Odom Prison, located in the northeastern part of the state, he spends his days learning gardening and woodworking. Because of his earlier affair with the jailer, his wife Kimberly filed for divorce shortly before Ronnie's trial began. Although she stood by Ronnie throughout his trial, she was noticeably absent at his sentencing hearing.

Because of their lack of prior serious criminal activity, Eric Thompson and Mike Melton received probation for their parts in the larcenies. Both young men testified for the prosecution at Ronnie's trial, both expressing their fear of Ted.

In July 1999, Reverend Ron Kimble Sr. resigned as pastor of Monnett Road Baptist Church. Throughout Ronnie's trial, attendance at the church fell, gradually dropping to only a handful of worshipers following Ted's confession. The former pastor and his wife Edna are now selling cotton candy and candy apples from a trailer they park in grocery-store parking lots. They still maintain their sons' innocence.

Sheila Blakley and Richard Blakley have put aside the bitterness of their divorce. Although they have no grave or memorial of Patricia to visit, they have their memories. "There isn't a day that goes by that I don't think of her," says Sheila. Richard is finally beginning to believe, and accept, that his daughter is never coming home. "For awhile," he says, "I would see someone in a crowd, just the back of their head, and maybe they had hair like Patricia, and I would think maybe—just maybe . . ."

In November 1998, Guilford County Sheriff B.J. Barnes was reelected by a landslide margin to his second term of office. Regarding the Kimble case, Barnes said, "There were no winners. It's a sad part of the county's history."

Detective Sergeant David DeBerry gave up making

the department's cakes but still enjoys baking cupcakes with his daughters. He's still searching for that prize-winning Mackerel and is planning on becoming a professional beach bum when he finally hangs up the badge and gun. Until then, he'll continue with the eighty-hour workweeks, the frustrations, and the satisfactions that come with being a homicide investigator.

Detective Jim Church still takes every off-duty assignment offered. He now has several homicide investigations under his belt, but none have had the effect of Patricia's. Says Church, "It was the case of a lifetime."

named Bambi and a kitten, Tigger, who rules the roost.

The author may be reached by E-mail at **LC396@aol.com**

ABOUT THE AUTHOR

Lynn Chandler-Willis is a native of North Carolina. She attended schools in Pleasant Garden and later attended Greensboro College.

In 1996, Chandler-Willis left corporate America and founded the Pleasant Garden Post, a biweekly newspaper, for which she is publisher and editor. The paper was a 1998 recipient of an Outstanding Community Service Award.

Prior to starting the newspaper, Chandler-Willis worked in merchandising at Wrangler Jeans, where she assisted in the design of women's blouses. She also was a production assistant for the nightly news at the ABC television news affiliate in High Point, North Carolina.

Chandler-Willis is a member of the Writer's Group of the Triad in North Carolina and also a member of the Mystery Writers of America. She continues to make her home in North Carolina with her son Garey and daughter Nina. The family also includes two Golden Retrievers, Brooks and Bailey; a poodle